More Houlihans
and
Horse Sense

Also by Vernon Schmid

Nonfiction
Northern Ireland: War and Peace in the Land of Saints and Scholars
The Power of the People (contributor)
Media and Methods for Your Church
Houlihans and Horse Sense
Cherokee Myth and Legend

Fiction
Seven Days of the Dog
Showdown at Chalk Creek
Watie's Wolves
Rags

Drama
Between Eleven and Thursday
One Night in Daylight
The Hare with Many Friends
Five Who Knew Jesus

Poetry
Poets and Priests and Madmen
Pilgrims
The Irish Poems
Of the Heart and the Bread (editor)
The Journey Toward
As Tentative as Flight (co-author)
Canonical Hours
Testament
Sleeping with Zapata
Hog Killers and Other Poems
Kissing Moctezuma's Serpent
Westering: New and Selected Poems, 1974–2004
Otium Sanctum: Poems for the Journey Toward

More Houlihans
and
Horse Sense

Vernon Schmid

iUniverse, Inc.

New York Lincoln Shanghai

More Houlihans and Horse Sense

iUniverse books may be ordered through booksellers or by contacting:

iUniverse
2021 Pine Lake Road, Suite 100
Lincoln, NE 68512
www.iuniverse.com
1-800-Authors (1-800-288-4677)

Because of the dynamic nature of the Internet, any Web addresses or links contained in this book may have changed since publication and may no longer be valid.

The views expressed in this work are solely those of the author and do not necessarily reflect the views of the publisher, and the publisher hereby disclaims any responsibility for them.
All of the pieces in this collection were published in their original form in the National Foundation Quarter Horse Journal, the Rising Sun (MD) Herald, the Herald County Edition, Roundup Magazine, and Country Magazine We are grateful for permission to reprint them.
Author photo credit—Ed Coburn

ISBN: 978-0-595-46909-3 (pbk)
ISBN: 978-0-595-91197-4 (ebk)

Printed in the United States of America

For Susan and All the Other Horse Sense Fans

"Every man has wanted to be a cowboy.
Why play Wall Street and die young
When you can play cowboy and never die?"

Will Rogers, July 10, 1931

Contents

Cowboys and Other Critters

Odds and Ends

Adios

Acknowledgements

All of the pieces in this collection were published in their original form in the National Foundation Quarter Horse Journal, the Rising Sun (MD) Herald, the Herald County Edition, Roundup Magazine, and Country Magazine We are grateful for permission to reprint them.

Preface

On a trip to Las Vegas to attend a meeting of the Western History Association, I met a cab driver from Philadelphia. We were having a nice chat about the mob in Philly on our way to the airport. He apparently had some minor "connections" years ago.

I told him about the "hit" that occurred shortly after Miss Susan and I and our daughters were transferred to the Philadelphia area. He knew about it. He said things were better in the old days when the mob just killed one another without involving innocent by-standers. Today, he said, the new gangs have no sense of responsibility they just shoot up neighborhoods injuring or killing innocent bystanders. Then, he said, "They're nothing but a bunch of cowboys."

Having pursued the cowboy way all my life and knowing a lot of real cowboys, that did not set well with me. I muttered to myself, "road apples," or something similar. But, I said nothing to him because I had been hearing those kinds of things most of my life and he might still have connections. It is a shame that "cowboy" seems to have become a popular pejorative term.

From my earliest childhood, all I ever wanted to be was a cowboy. From my first horse when I was seven until the present day, the cowboy culture has fascinated me. From my days eating arena dust on the rodeo circuit as a passable bareback bronc rider to cleaning up road apples around our place, the sense that I have remained true to the cowboy code has prevailed in my life.

Folks continually ask me how I remain so cowboy in outlook, dress, manner and attitude and live in Maryland. In fact, a writer friend, Don Coldsmith, described me in one of his syndicated columns as a true westerner, a cowboy who "for some obscure reason lives in Maryland."

Don knows what a lot of we westerners know. Being western has nothing to do with geography. It has to do with what is implanted in your bones, what kind of dirt is beneath your nails, or as one writer explained it, "what kind of dirt you've tasted."

I once explained to a friend that I could not write fiction or poetry about the Chesapeake Bay region, although I have lived there for over twenty-five years. I simply cannot feel what you have to feel about a place to write honestly about it.

That is to say, being western is more than the way you dress. It is easy to try to dress like a cowboy. You can buy the clothing almost everywhere. A lot of it is what they call retro. It looks like the junk they used to wear in all those old singing cowboy movies. I knew even way back when I went to see those movies on Saturday that real cowboys do not wear embroidered shirts even though they do have spurs that jingle-jangle as they go riding along.

You can buy boots with silver tips on them (no real cowboy would be caught dead in them) and hats with fancy bands, but that does not make you a cowboy. Being westerner requires roots. It has to do with mixing the sweat of horses and cows and working men and women to make a soup that stands up and talks back, that reveals the heart of a westerner.

With that said, I acknowledge that I know westerners who happen to live in the east. Some haven't been west much but they have soaked up the essence of the cowboy life and know something that is inexplicable to other folks. It has to do with how you treat others, how you treat livestock, how you sit your saddle, how you have come to know the moon and stars, the setting sun.

Therefore, on the flight home from Las Vegas, I thought about the cab driver's remark and remembered something from the old days: Gene Autry's Cowboy Code. It goes like this:

> The Cowboy must never shoot first, hit a smaller man, or take unfair advantage.
> The Cowboy must never go back on his word, or a trust confided in him.
> The Cowboy must always tell the truth.
> The Cowboy must be gentle with children, the elderly, and animals.
> The Cowboy must not advocate or possess racially or religiously intolerant ideas.
> The Cowboy must help people in distress.
> The Cowboy must be a good worker.
> The Cowboy must keep himself clean in thought, speech, action, and personal habits.
> The Cowboy must respect women, parents, and his nation's laws.
> The Cowboy is a patriot.

I think Gene had it right. We need more real cowboys in the world. I was thinking about all of that while I was driving down the highway with a horse trailer hanging on behind my pick-em-up-truck praying I wouldn't make another sharp turn and smash up it the side again. My head was in the clouds as usual, and I paying little attention to my driving, when the idea struck me again.

Why not gather some more the columns and articles and put them into another collection for the folks who tell me they missed that one or this one?

I did that with some of them in a little book called **Houlihans and Horse Sense** a few years ago. That was in the beginning and a lot more stuff has evolved out of my distancing myself from physical labor, combined with sitting and sunning half-a-sleep in a chair on the back porch or daydreaming while I drive or ride my old mare at a slow walk through meadows and fields. Therefore, I have taken some of the most popular pieces published in the past few years (one's folks have really responded to) and put them together. Hope you get a kick out of **More Houlihans and Horse Senses**.

—Vernon Schmid

Horses and Such

A Matter of Survival

In *Bite the Bullet,* one of my all-time favorite western movies, a cowboy played by Gene Hackman is discussing a 700 mile race that is at the center of the story. He explains to another competitor that a horse will run itself to death just to please its rider. He says, "a horse don't give a damn who wins."

That's the truth. Horses run because it is the nature of a prey animal like a horse to be fleet of foot to escape predators. It is part of the genetic make-up of horse. However, running is not a matter of winning but just being able to elude the pursuer. The most natural way to run is in a herd. Therefore, that is what is happening when the gates open at a racetrack and the horses charge around the track.

My old friend Bill owns Thoroughbreds he races. It probably disturbs him to know that horses don't care who wins. From what he has told me, his horses really do not care. But, the maintenance, care, and training of a race horse is designed to keep this instinct pent-up, so that when the opportunity comes to lay back their ears and run flat out is in fact an emotional release, as much as anything else.

Animal behavioral scientists have studied racehorses and they have come up with some interesting observations. The first is the simple fact that it is unnatural for horses to run at high speed over long distances.

No wild horse would ever run at top speed without being in a state of complete panic. Normally when trying to evade a predator the herd moves at a brisk trot. Only if the predator is visible and attacking would the horse break into full gallop. Somewhere, in the racehorse's mind there is instilled a fantasy of a pursuing killer. And the whip jockeys use must recall from ancient genetic make-up the pain of a predator's claws from which to escape.

So, as the horses burst from the gate in a thundering herd it is just possible that they are simply physically expressing themselves after long periods of restraint and confinement. And maybe, Bill, the character in the movie is right. The horse doesn't care who wins, he just runs because he likes to run.

About Horses

I confess I have always been a fan of William Shakespeare. That's right! And I listen to classical music while driving my old pick-em-up truck! So, there!

In King Henry V, Act 3, Shakespeare has his character say, "I will not change my horse with any that treads ... When I bestride him, I soar, I am a hawk. He trots the air; the earth sings when he touches it." That kind of love brings a tear to eye of horse lovers.

In the same play Billy Shakespeare writes, "He is pure air and fire; and the dull elements of earth and water never appear in him, but only in patient stillness while his rider mounts him; he is indeed a horse, and all other jades, you may call beasts."

Being more grounded in reality there is an old Yiddish proverb that draft horses will relate to as soon as they know how to read: "The wagon rests in winter, the sleigh in summer, the horse never."

One of Shakespeare's compatriots, Ben Johnson (not the cowboy actor, the English writer), had this to say about horses.

"They say princes learn no art truly, but the art of horsemanship. The reason is, the brave beast is no flatterer. He will throw a prince as soon as his groom."

Now that's a true saying.

I am also a great fan of the Marx brothers. I have watched their films hundreds of times and laugh aloud at every joke I know by heart. In "A Day at the Races" Groucho says to the leading lady, "Marry me and I'll never look at another horse." Now, that is a real kicker!

Being a reformed high school drop out I connect with Charles Caleb Colton's remark, "To sentence a man of true genius to the drudgery of a school is to put a racehorse on a treadmill."

A Russian proverb helps us know how important proper feed is to the life of a horse. It goes like this: "It is not the horse that draws the cart, but the oats."

And those who have lived their lives with horses know this statement by Alois Podhajsky in "My Horses, My Teachers" is true.

"My horses not only taught me riding, but they also made me understand many a wisdom of life besides."

There's a cute saying by jockey Angel Cordero, Jr.; "If it has four legs, and I'm riding it, I think I can win."

I can't end this without offending someone, so here's a quote from Christopher Morley.

"Few girls are as well shaped as a horse."

On a serious note, there is an old English saying that goes like this: "Show me your horse and I will tell you who you are."

Finally, on a spiritual note, "After God, we owe it all to horses."

An Arabian Moment

The closest I ever got to Arabs was a few years ago on a fact-finding mission in the Middle East. I spent about ten of days in a two-week span in the company of Palestinian Arabs., the other days with Israeli officials. I wore a *kafiyah*, ate *falafel*, and rode a camel on the side of the hill overlooking the Garden of Gethsemane. The hill was called the Mount of Olives. I even went to a party where Arab food was served, Arab music was played and the daughter of our hosts danced some Arabian folk dances for us. However, I never knew much about Arabian horses.

Out of ignorance, I always treated the whole concept of Arabian horses with less than enthusiasm. That's how most folks deal with the unknown. We ridicule it, hate it, or remain suspicious of it. Oh, I knew they were beautiful. That little dish in their face and the way they carried their tail, sort of like a flag, was always a remarkable sight. I also knew that they were foundation stock for Spanish Barb horses and Thoroughbreds way back in the past. But, one thing was certain, I had never ridden one.

Then, a few summers ago my neighbor Jan Zook invited me to a gymkhana and loaned me her black Egyptian mare, Zee. It was my first time aboard an Arabian and we even picked up some ribbons. Therefore, along with my neighbor having Arabians and a few of my students at the time at Cecil Community College owning Arabians, I took a closer look at them.

At the 2000 World Horse Expo in Timonium, Maryland, I met Lisa and Don Stepler of Double S Arabians south of Elkton, Maryland. Their stallion Nonsuch Padron, a class A halter and liberty champion, was absolutely gorgeous. The son of a world champion, he gives meaning to the word class. Therefore, as I move about and meet more and more horses, some with owners attached, I continue to be impressed by the beauty and grace of Arabians. Sitting on my deck a while back I glanced through the pines towards my neighbor's pasture and watched her Arabians move across the landscape and even though I remain a Quarter Horse man, I do have Arabian moments.

Bi-lingual Appaloosa

A rancher friend of mine used to rent horses to dudes for trail rides. He lived along the Colorado-New Mexico border most of his life and speaks both English and a little Spanish. One summer, while I was there, he went to lunch at a Mexican restaurant with his wife and came back just in time to instruct a large family of Italians how to ride their horses in the Wild West. The problem was the Italians did not understand English. Therefore, the instructions were hard to communicate. However, eventually the wrangler led them away on their trail ride and my old friend stood there with a big smile on his face.

"You know," he said, "after one shot of tequila I am tri-lingual. No telling how many languages I could speak if I drank a whole bottle of the stuff."

Well, my experience with tequila leads me to believe that tequila doesn't teaches you much of any thing except how to make a fool out of yourself. However, language is a funny thing.

Violating the Quarter Horse code, Miss Susan has an Appaloosa mare. One weekend, we discovered something significant. Her Appaloosa is bi-lingual and she doesn't even drink tequila.

You see, Dorothee, a friend of hers, came to visit and went for a ride. She groomed the mare, tacked her up and got on board. She began to ride the old Appy around in the pasture and then it happened. I heard her giving commands to the mare—in French.

You see, Miss Susan's friend is French Canadian. She migrated from Montreal to serve as the reference library's supervisor at the public library. The neat thing is, if someone calls about something French, or speaks French, she is right on. Of course, there is little call locally for a French-speaking librarian. In fact, English, for some of us, is difficult. But, apparently there is a need for a French speaking horsewoman.

The old Appy gets a little stubborn sometimes. She doesn't like to work. Like a lot of cayuses, and a lot of human beans, she would rather build her daily life around eating. Every time she would falter that day, or try to take a different route than the one her rider wanted, Dorothee would mutter something in French. The old mare would respond with a toss of her head and an occasional snort. Then, as if she understood completely what was being said to her, she would obey and strike out in that long legged, high stepping Indian shuffle gait she has.

Now, I know horses probably do not understand precisely what we are saying. I don't even understand what I am saying, half of the time. And I know horses probably aren't really bi-lingual. But, I also know what I saw and heard. So, all of my presumptions may be way off base.

Whatever was happening that day the old mare understood. So, I prefer to think of her as bi-lingual. And Miss Susan is proud to be the owner of a bi-lingual horse.

Camping Out in the Barn

Miss Susan had nothing to do with my moving to the barn Memorial Day week-end in 2006. I chose to do that on my own when our Quarter Horse mare, BH High Hopes a.k.a Ginger, started showing signs of imminent delivery. Now, I gave up camping out a long time ago, but I was concerned about her. She was twenty-one years old and a maiden when we bred her, so we wanted to have an eye on her at delivery time.

Ginger and I settled in. The bullfrogs in the pond behind our place were sounding off like the Mormon Tabernacle Choir, their rhythmic croak lulling me to sleep. I would doze in the chair in the barn runway until Ginger moved and my eyes would pop open. About 10 p.m., some yahoo down the road started setting off fireworks like it was a Chinese New Year. It startled Ginger to say nothing of me. We finally settled down and since I was wide-awake, I stepped outside and looked up at the sky. It was clear and every star, planet, and pocket of gas was brilliant.

The Big Dipper hung over head and I spent some time just looking at it. In the distance, the Milky Way was flung across the sky. According to my Cherokee ancestors, the Big Dipper is called "The Boys" and the Milky Way is called "Where the Dog Ran."

It seems that when the world was new, seven boys would rather play ball with sticks and a stone instead of working. Their mothers scolded them and then collected stones, boiled them in a pot with corn for dinner. When the boys came home hungry, their mothers dipped out the stone soup for their supper. The boys grew angry and danced their way into the heavens where they are known by many names including the Pleiades, the Seven Sisters, and the Big Dipper.

As far as the Milky Way goes, every day old women ground fresh cornmeal, only to have it stolen at night by a dog. The old women waited one night and caught the dog in the act. They whipped him and he ran howling home to the north, leaving tracks to trace his path across a darkened sky, his mouth-dropping evidence of the robbery. Therefore, the Cherokee call the Milky Way, "Where the Dog Ran."

Back in the barn, it eventually became clear this might not be the night, but I stayed just in case. Finally, a 4 a.m., I was seeing double and headed for the house for relief. Miss Susan took over and let me sleep for a few hours. I woke up to find that she had fed the horses, swept the barn runway and cleaned the stalls. As Yoda the Jedi Master would say, "Good help, she is." I add, "Good friend, she is."

After a late breakfast, we groomed Ginger and used a little fly spray to make her more comfortable. Then Bill Hentosh, photographer for Country magazine, came by and took some pictures. Our story about the birth was scheduled for publication in the August/September issue. He hoped the foal would be here, but alas, she was not. He would return later for pictures of the baby.

After he left, Miss Susan and I took turns checking on Ginger while our neighbor Jan and farrier friend Tommy kept in touch. They seemed as anxious as we did about the impending change in our lives.

Ginger was perspiring heavily and her discomfort greatly increased at 2 a.m. the next morning. The foal was getting ready and so was Ginger. The contractions began and we started calling folks who left word to do just that. Our vet, Dr. Joe Haines, thanked us and told us to keep him informed of the progress, rolled over and being an intelligent man, I presume he went back to sleep. Our neighbor Jan was awake when we called and she came down the hill to our place. The next call was to our friend Tom. Now, you must understand that we called Tom at 2 a.m. just to be ornery. But, lo and behold, he and wife Pat arrived fifteen minutes later.

By 2:40 Ginger was in full-blown labor and after some struggle, she delivered at 2:55. The foal emerged properly like a diver, front legs and head emerging together. Both mare and foal were fine. I cleared the baby's breathing passage, removed the placenta from her body and began drying her with a towel while Ginger engaged in the same process with her tongue. Thus began what is known as imprinting. That is, the foal would connect to the ones she first encounters.

Miss Susan's sister, Barbara, lives in Wyoming. She was visiting in Kansas and had been calling us every few hours to inquire about the birth. Therefore, I called her at 3 a.m. (that's 2 a.m. in Kansas). She woke up, sleepily answered the phone, and groaned, "Good," when I told we had a new baby girl. Then, she hung up. Or, at least I think she did. Everything went silent on the other end.

The morning crowd grew but Ginger took it all in stride and like the proud mother she is she let folks ooh and aw over the new baby.

Our Quarter Horse breeding and training friends, Keith, Mary Ann and Jim arrived. They stayed for a spell looking at the new foal and new horse trailer and then left to go haul and store 1700 bales of hay. Neighbors Tom and Grace showed up with a container filled with breakfast—sausage, bacon, eggs, hash browns, a biscuit and two glazed cinnamon rolls. We ate and went back to barn just as our other neighbors, Ed and Debbie, showed up with a Breyers model foal as a birthday gift.

Exhausted, Miss Susan and I took turns staying at the barn and going to the house to cleanup. Then Bill Hentosh was back on site taking pictures as Dr. Haines arrived and pronounced mother and baby in excellent condition.

With company gone, we all began to relax. Miss Susan made potato salad and deviled eggs for a Memorial Day dinner. We grilled some burgers and bratwurst and sat down to eat. Our oldest daughter, Susanna, came to take photos and joined us. Other neighbors dropped by and asked if they could see the foal. While they leaned on the fence looking at mother and daughter, we ate our dinner and watched them through the kitchen window. When we finished we went out to visit with them before I took Ginger and the foal back to the barn for the night.

The miracle of birth remains just that and the excitement that surrounds it is well founded. Camping out in the barn was worth it.

Common Sense

I was sitting in the office of Southfork Stables in Durango, Colorado, back in 1999, when a young woman came in to register for a trail ride. She said she was an experienced rider. That is usually a clue that they aren't. She was also a fan of Pat Parelli from Pagosa Springs just down the road. She signed up for a ride, paid the boss and then asked a leading question.

"What do you think of Pat Parelli's training methods?"

The boss, a long time cowboy, breeder and horse trainer, never dropped a beat. "Hell," he said, "it's just common sense."

I thought about that comment as I sat down to write this column. I've written about the subject before but a reminder is always good. Therefore, let's discuss "etiquette" for equestrians. In my circle of friends, the French word "etiquette" translates to "common sense." One thing is necessary. Make sure that old pony you ride has the disposition and training to be ridden on public trails, many of which are congested. If your horse has some tendencies that make it an undesirable on the trail warn others. They have a ribbon system (red on the tail for a kicker, yellow for a stallion). The best thing is to simply tell (split infinitive) folks to keep their distance, or at least inform them of your horse's bad habits. That said, sometimes the unexpected still happens.

When I was trail guide in Colorado, we always had a slicker tied behind the cantle of the clients' saddle. On a switch back trail up the side of a mesa, I looked back o see one of my "dudes" on a gentle old bay in the process of trying not to get bucked off. The yellow slicker came untied and was flapping on one side of then horse who came undone, as well. I could not get back down the trail to help the rider. When he simply stepped off the horse at a high place along the trail and held him until he quieted and the walked up the trail to where we could retie the slicker. We were lucky. The rider was a Chicago mounted police officer on vacation. He knew what to do and how to do it. That isn't often true.

And for crying out loud, obey posted signs and gait limits. This goes back to my first statement about common sense. Doing silly things like galloping on a busy trail pouts everyone in danger including you. If someone is passing move to the right and let them pass. If you are passing, move to the left. I was going to say just like you drive, but I've seen some of you drive, so I'll let that pass.

Be courteous. If you are going to turn, or slow down, duck a branch, tell folks behind you. I like to bend the branch and let it slap the rider behind me in the face, but that ain't good. Remember, many folks out of the trail are novices. Some just got a horse yesterday and are lucky to know how to groom and saddle.

Finally, if you trailer, and most of us do, don't clean the trailer out in the parking area. Use "common sense," or as my daddy used to say," horse sense."

Changing Horse Populations

Reports have revealed some interesting facts about horses nationwide. A decade or so ago, the Quarter Horse led the pack in foal crop size. In second place were Thoroughbreds with Arabians in third place. In the top ten Appaloosas were fourth in foal crop size followed by Standardbreds, Paints, Anglo and Half Arabians, Tennessee Walking Horses, Morgans and Saddlebreds. But things have changed.

Quarter Horses still hold first place in the number of foals this past year, but Paints are now in second place. Thoroughbreds have dropped to third and Tennessee Walking Horses have moved into fourth place. Arabians and Standardbreds are tied in fifth position for the number of foals dropped. Appaloosas have come in sixth and Miniature Horses, which weren't even in the 1980's now, have the seventh highest new foal registration volume. I wonder where they get all the little people to ride those ponies. In eighth place are Anglo and Half-Arabians and Morgans and Racking Horses at the bottom of the list in the top ten.

Paints have grown by leaps and bounds in popularity in the last quarter of a century. They added 62,000 registered foals to their list just last year. In 1998 the only registered 55,356 and back in 1975 there were only 5,896 foals registered. Expectations are that over a 100,000 will be registered in the coming year of two. That will make the annual Paint foal crop larger than breeds three through ten combined.

Paints have come a long way since I was riding my paint horse in the Colorado Rockies fifty years ago. Old Duke was the only one in the upper Arkansas Valley and we got to show off a lot. But, times change and so have the tastes of horse folks, as recent statistics show us.

Imprinted

I had been standing astride our two-week-old foal for several days while I inserted a tube into her mouth to administer a small dosage of medication designed to balance her digestive system. She was used to this and offered no resistance. One day, however, just as I finished she bounced to one side in a fit of youthful joy, upset my aging balance and down we went. I bumped my head as I hit the ground with her laying on one of my legs. Her mother whuffled a little and stood looking at both of us as if to say, "What are you guys doing now."

Jazzy leaped to her feet, sped off across the paddock, slid to a stop and turned to look back at me sitting on the ground. I must have had a look of shock and surprise on my face. She stood watching me while I sat contemplating what had just happened. This gentle little foal had dumped me and I wasn't even wearing spurs or actually sitting on her back. So, there I was sitting on the ground in the middle of the corral looking puzzled and embarrassed when Old Beans came driving up in his battered Ford pick-em-up-truck. He opened the door, got out, and walked over to the fence and stood leaning on it and staring at me.

"What are you doing sitting on the ground?" he asked.

"Got bucked off."

"Bucked off? At your age you ought to know better," he said.

"Well," I replied as I slowly got up, "I apparently have not learned that lesson yet."

"What happened?"

"I been imprinting the new foal," I said. "And I was just doctoring her a little."

He snorted and as I turned to walk away, he remarked, "From looks of the grass stains on your rump, I'd say she imprinted you."

"Yeah," I said. "But, we are still getting along just fine."

"Sure looks it," he said with a chuckle and turned to walk away.

"Where are you going?" I asked.

"Gonna go have a cup of coffee at the truck stop," he said as he got into his truck. "And besides, I don't want to hang around here and watch you getting imprinted again."

Having a newborn horse on the property is a lot like having a new child. She is curious, tastes everything, and runs like the wind, bucks, kicks, and whinnies. When I go to feed her mother in the morning, she is standing at the stall door waiting to be let out for another run.

I called the stallion owner in Joseph, Oregon, the other day and caught him off guard when I asked, "Brent, do you guarantee live foals?"

There was a pause on his end of the line and he said, "Oh, my! What happened?"

I said, "Nothing happened. I just called to tell you she is REALLY alive!"

He laughed and I pictured him picking himself up off the floor after my initial question. I did not tell him she had imprinted me.

Eat, Sleep and Cavort

I looked out the kitchen window one day and saw Rags Bandy standing out by my barn leaning on a corral fence. I stepped out on the porch and yelled at him.

"What are doing out there?"

"Just looking at your new foal," he said.

"Not gonna steal her are you?' I asked.

"Nope. Just considering."

"Considering what?"

"Considering whether or not I believe in reincarnation."

"Do you?"

"Don't know. But, I'm thinking on it."

"Look at her," he said. "All she does is eat, sleep and cavort. That's the life I want to live."

"We did once," I said.

"Maybe when we were young, but we grew out of it," he said.

"So will she," I said.

"That's why I'm thinking about reincarnation," he grinned. "Pour me a cup of coffee and I will elucidate."

"Elucidate? What are you talking about?"

"Just pour the coffee and I will explain it to you."

I led the way into the kitchen and poured him a cup of coffee. He sat down at the table and gazed pout the window at the frolicking foal.

"You see," he began. "Incarnation means you never die. You just pass on into some other living creature or thing."

I stared at him for a moment before speaking.

"You've been reading again, haven't you?" I said.

"Pay attention," he said. "Don't try to distract me."

I sipped my coffee and looked at him over the rim of the cup.

"When you die and they bury you, flowers grow on your grave. They are alive and you are contained in them. Get it?"

"Yep," I said.

"So we never really pass out of the world we just change shape, or form, or species."

"You really have been reading, haven't you? Where did you pick up the word species?"

"There you go again, trying to distract. Now pay attention. I want to come back as a foal and do nothing by eat, sleep and cavort."

"What are you going to do when you grow up?" I asked.

"Ain't gonna grow up," he said. "Just when it looks like I'm gonna to grow up I'll die and come back as another foal."

"More likely you'll be a flower and a horse will come along and eat you. Then you'll pass through his body and fall on the ground to fertilize other flowers and you may never get another chance to eat, sleep and cavort."

"I never thought of that," he said as he gazed out the window. "But, just look at her cavort.

First Horse

The first horse is always a wondrous experience. I have written before about Charlie, my first horse. He was white, blind and beautiful. My father got him in a multiple horse-trading deal. He brought him home, handing his lead rope to me and said," There. Now you can quite begging for a horse."

I did. My first horse and I connected in such a way that trust bonded us. I would never hurt him. He would never hurt me. I don't remember how old he was. I know I was eight. We worked together and we played together. From day to day, I was a cowboy, but mostly I was Indian. I had no saddle. Didn't need one. I climbed up on fences, hay racks, whatever to get aboard and once aboard I stayed. Charlie and I would disappear in the back pasture out of reach my father's voice calling me.

Thinking about this while visiting with some ranchers in a cafe out west this spring, the subject of horse training came up. As we talked, I told them about a training method I discovered some years ago. It had to do with how some Plains Indian tribes would connect a first horse and young rider in a spiritual way.

When it came time for the boy to get his first horse the family would present him with a horse on a long lead. They would tie the lead around the boy's waist and the horse and the boy would go away together for a few days. It was a lesson for both. Each would get to know the other by being unable to function without the other. In a sense, they became spiritually connected by being physically connected.

Later some horse trainers began using the same method in a corral and even later in a round pen. They would simply sit on a chair or up-turned bucket for a day with the horse loose in the corral doing what it would normally do. It became become accustomed to the presence of the trainer and the trainer would "get to know the horse."

I still do that a lot. Just sit with my horse and feel the spiritual connection between us. It's a good feeling and a good practice. I recommend it.

Foundation Quarter Horses

When I had the opportunity to spend time with the editorial staff of the National Foundation Quarter Horse Journal a magazine that carries this column, they treated Miss Susan and me real well. They even fed us one night. Like any carnivore, my heart belongs to the one who feeds me. While we visited, I asked them about the history of the organization that publishes the magazine: The National Foundation Quarter Horse Association (NFQHA).

Now, I know some things about it. I am, after all, a life member. Nevertheless, the reason for its founding was interesting. It seems that over a decade ago, some Quarter Horse owners started discussing the fact that so many Quarter Horses had been out bred to Thoroughbreds so long that they were loosing their original distinctive Quarter Horse traits: beautiful heads, strong chests and hips, intelligence and a quiet disposition, among others. The question was how do we determine just how much of a Quarter Horse is a Quarter Horse?

They hit on the idea of research and came up with a computer software system that plugs into the American Quarter Horse Association (AQHA) data bank and determines how much "foundation" blood a horse has. They then began to certify horses that were 80% or higher as foundation Quarter Horses. The horses have to be registered with the AQHA before they can be certified with NFQHA. And like the AQHA, the owner has to join the NFQHA to have their horse certified. The idea took off.

These days they have over 30,000 registered Quarter Horses certified in their own data bank. I took the leap a few years ago and discovered that, BH High Hopes aka Ginger, my old mare is 99% foundation bred. She has a lot of King Ranch breeding, the only significant Thoroughbreds in her ancestry is King Plaudit and Lani Chief, and they are a long way back.

For those who love Quarter Horses, like me, it is nice to know that you have the real thing under saddle and not a Thoroughbred wannabe Quarter Horse. How's that for snobbery.

Get a Rope

A reader called me one day. A horsewoman who occasionally offers free leases, or loans her horses to other folks so the horse will be used. A while back, she loaned a bay Arabian stallion to another woman for use at her stable and for shows. Since the woman was going to show the horse she also loaned her the horse's registration papers.

A few months later, she received a call from yet another woman who now possessed the horse. It seems she wanted the owner to come sign the registration papers so an official transfer could be recorded. When questioned the woman who bought the horse said, "No, he isn't a stallion. He is a one-eyed gelding."

The woman who called me made a hasty trip to the Pennsylvania home of the person who now had the horse only to be told that the horse was in training in Virginia. But, would she please sign the registration papers? Our reader looked at the papers, and, "Yes," it was the same horse.

Of course, her answer was a resounding "No!" She would not sign the transfer papers. And besides how did she get the horse?

She bought it, the new owner said, at a horse auction.

The reader asked what my thoughts were on the situation. I suggested that a written contract would have helped, if not absolutely necessary. But, coming from the west, my first reaction was "Get a rope!"

You see, in the old west horses were essential not only for transportation but for economic survival. Therefore, it was a hanging offense to steal someone's horse. We don't do that anymore, even in the west. Nevertheless, western states require more than a Coggins and a health certificate for owner transfer. Most western states require a Department of Agriculture inspection of the animal, called a brand inspection, before the horse can moved across a state line and, in some cases, out of the county. They call the guys who do that "Brand Inspectors."

Ownership transfer of a horse is one thing, and I didn't think I would ever say this, they make too easy in the east. It is no wonder more things like this don't happen where a simple bill of sale suffices.

Needless to say, the reader filed criminal charges where the present possessor of the Arabian lives and where the original lessee lives. One can only hope there is some recourse.

Hitched on Horseback

Sam and Darcy of Blue Goose Stables, Cochranville, Pennsylvania, are team ropers. And they wanted to get married on their roping horses. So, they asked around and a mutual acquaintance told them to give me a call. They did and we connected.

Well, cowboy type weddings are old hat to me, so we did it up right. We met at Maryland's Fair Hill Natural Resources Center for rehearsal and a couple of hours of trail riding. Then two days later the bride, mounted on a paint gelding, wore a half-veil and was accompanied by four maids of honor. They were all students at Blue Goose Stables and wore matching shirts with their English riding attire. The groom was cleaned up pretty good, as well, and riding his dun roping horse.

I liked doing this because it gives me a chance to dude it up. I wore my black flat brimmed, open crown hat; black high topped Olathe boots with big-roweled Mexican spurs and rode my chestnut Quarter Horse mare, Ginger.

The ceremony took place on a hilltop with a broad vista of woods and rolling hills. The crowd of family and friends were trucked in and stood or sat while the bride's son played the bride into the place on his electric battery powered keyboard.

There was a little breeze and Ginger and the bride's horse got into a tiny little disagreement over who was charge, but otherwise the wedding went off like clockwork. Then the bride and groom kissed, turned their horses and rode away followed by the four attendants. The mounted entourage circled the wedding guests twice and the cantered off into the distance and out of sight.

Best wishes went out to them. They are good people and may they keep riding on.

Hollywood Dun It, Done It!

A lot has been written about the late Hollywood Dun It, the first American Quarter Horse and National Foundation Quarter Horse whose offspring earned more than $4 million. The stallion won the National Reining Horse Association (NRHA) Futurity, Derby, and Superstakes, National Reining Breeders Classic, All American Quarter Horse Congress Futurity, Southwest Reining Horse Association Futurity, Tradition Futurity, and numerous others. He earned over $100,000 in performance and sire awards. His offspring are big stoppers, deadly leaded, and nimble turners.

Much of the appeal of Hollywood Dun It and his offspring was that they are affectionate, intelligent and talented—it is a great combination. He produced American Quarter Horse Association World Champions and multiple NRHA World and Reserve World Champions and was selected the first Breyer Animal Creations reining horse in 1998.

However, it was the horse, himself, who touched people. Daily, they came to Tioga, Texas from all over the world to visit this fabulous dun stallion. Part of it was that unforgettable face—the kind eye and sculpted head that he passes on to his children.

He was also a "people" horse that loved to play to a crowd. Years ago, his charisma resulted in winning performances. A bow for a carrot captured hearts. It is his picture, however, that played a role in a Maryland teenager's life.

Rick Devine was a horseman. His grandmother, Jan Zook, brought up her children to love horses and her grandchildren in the same manner. Along the way, Rick got a beautiful classic buckskin Quarter Horse mare named Moneys Fancy Face (a.k.a Fancy) and was winning ribbons with her. Then, one day, driving home from a store, Rick hit a tree. Suffering significant brain damage, he was unconscious and not expected to live. And this is where Hollywood Dun It came into the picture.

His grandmother went to the hospital where they prayed he would regain consciousness. She brought a copy of the Quarter Horse Journal with Hollywood Dun It's beautiful head on the cover. She held the magazine up to Rick's unseeing eyes that were closed.

"Ricky," she said. "I found a boyfriend for Fancy." He slowly opened his eyes and looked at the picture.

Rick is twenty-two now. Still confined to a wheelchair, he has made a lot of progress over the years. He can eat again without being fed through a tube in his stomach. He talks little, but smiles a lot. He is using one arm more and more. He has done some therapeutic riding with help from volunteers, attends play days a local saddle club puts on and watches with great interest.

His grandmother says, without equivocation, Tim McQuay does not know that the greatest thing Hollywood Dun It ever did was bring a boy back to life.

And by the way, Fancy had a foal by I Am A Dun Cody, a son of Hollywood Dun It.

Horses

No matter how old I get, no matter where I live, horses fascinate me. It all began with my daddy.

He was my first hero. He left home when he was twelve to work on a farm. With little formal education, he came to know horses and cattle, was a good farrier and a tricky horse trader. He was nothing like the cowboys I saw on the Saturday movie screens, but he knew and loved good horses.

I still watch every cowboy movie I can, although Miss Susan keeps telling me, "You know that film by heart." I explain to her that it is not the movie, it is not even the actors, it is the horses. I watch cowboy movies to see horses and scenery.

Ever since I rode the grass on our lawn down to dust on a self-made stick horse, the affinity for horses has prevailed in my heart and soul. Daddy got my first horse in a multi-horse swap when I was seven. It became an extension of my life. Even in times when I could not own a horse, they were never far from my mind. Just ask my wife, my daughters, family and friends. Driving down highways I lose all thought of driving when I see horses along the road. I stare at them, make comments about them, judge them, name their breed, remark on how they are cared for and I am constantly being told to watch the road, not the horses.

One thing that stays with me is my experience with horses. They inform me. They teach me. They relate to me with sound and movement. They tell me things humans cannot know or express. My old foundation Quarter Horse mare is a good example.

She communicates with me. We are both getting up in years and I am convinced she knows that. She plays with me and let's me know when I'm a little tardy with the feed. I awaken many mornings and tromp down the stairs to see her staring at the kitchen window waiting for some sign of life. As soon as she sees it, she whinnies. Miss Susan laughs and says things like, "You better get out there and feed her before she comes up here and gets you."

Horse folk know what I am talking about. Horses may have biologically small brains, but they have excellent memories. In addition, my old mare has that natural Quarter Horse calmness. A trainer once used her to show folks at a clinic how a horse should behave. He said, "This mare knows more about being a horse than anyone can teach her." Nice compliment.

I think Will Rogers said it best back 1932 when he wrote, "There will never be a time when the old horse is not superior to any auto ever made."

Horses Ain't Easy to Love

I have written about my horse rancher friends out in the San Juan Mountains of southwest Colorado before. Well, a while back it seems they had a rough summer. First, the fires all around the region killed the tourist trade they depend on for the summer months. The rent horses and guide folks on rides through the mountains. This year times were pretty rough, but they got rougher.

Kim, she's the pretty one in the crowd and a good horse trainer and team roper, was participating in the annual Fourth of July parade in Durango when a little girl's pony kicked her and shattered her fibula. That put her down for the summer and fall and by winter and she was still stumping around on what she called her Herman Munster boot.

The next day Ol' Rick, a former rodeo rough stock rider, bucked off a colt, broke four ribs and punctured a lung. Instead of naming a wing after them the hospital kept him overnight, then re-admitted him 2 days later with pneumonia! Rick healed and went back to guiding elk and deer hunters up in the San Juans. Their teen age son, Coleman, became known around town as the "Last Baird Standing."

Horses will do that to you. These folks spend everyday of their lives with horses and have all their life. Rick wrangled horses with his dad on the set of the Jimmy Stewart-Audie Murphy movie "Night Passage." He was the little boy that crossed the street in front of Stewart when he got off the train.

Kim is a skilled horse trainer who grew up in the ranch business and knows more about horses than most anyone. But, in a millisecond a horse can be seriously injure you. Hey, after all they weigh a thousand pounds or more. Sometimes they ain't easy to love. Horse folk know this, but they accept the inherent danger.

Horses ain't easy to love, but doggone it they are pure delight. So, take a lesson from the Bairds and keep your eyes open and your wits about you as you ride on.

Horse Lingo

While on a book-signing trip in Missouri, Kansas and Oklahoma, I was reminded of how much pride people take in their horses. For instance, any back highway in eastern Oklahoma will reveal horses everywhere. On small plots of land like my own or sprawling ranches, horses are clearly visible. Folks love them and take pride in announcing to the passing traveler, "See my horses."

It got me to thinking about how horse-folk talk about their animals, cowboys used to refer to them as their "mounts." It did not matter if he had two or eight. They were collectively called "mounts" or in the case of a working cowboy his "string."

The working cowboy had to have a good string. He used them daily. He had morning horses, afternoon horses, cutting horses, a special horse for night hawking, etc. Together these strings made up something called a remuda from the Spanish *remonta*.

Cowboys in different parts of the country called horses by different names. A mustang was a wild horse of unmixed wild horse heritage. Cowboys for a couple of reasons never used most of these. First, they were hard to catch and secondly, unless you caught one before the age of two it was unlikely they would ever be useful working cattle. The standard belief was they would always be trying to escape and go back to the wild bunch.

Wild horses in Oregon country were called "cayuses" after the Cayuse Indians, who, by the way, were excellent horse people. It is they, along with the Nez Perce and Palouse, who developed the Appaloosa.

Bronco was a name also given to wild or semi-tame horses. Sometimes shortened to bronc it came from the Spanish term *broncho* meaning rude or rough. And all those western novels that talked about a cowboy getting on his bronco and riding into the sunset are just silly. Cowboys were not into riding rude horses.

And the word pony had nothing to do with size. In the northwestern part of the country, the word pony was used many times instead of horse, as in cow pony. Speaking of cow ponies, a good cow pony had one eye on the cow and one on the ground. Some say they are born that way. That is, the horses are bred, like my old mare, in such a way as to make them natural cow ponies. My mare comes from a long line of famous King Ranch stallions whose sole purpose was to produce horses with cow sense. She will herd anything, cows, horses, or people.

Well, enough about lingo. Check your cinch and ride on.

Horse Radar

I have big ears, but my daddy had really big ears. But, both of us had a little hearing problem, as we got older. Being hit just above the ear with a horse's hoof causes mine. I don't know why he had problems. He spent a lot of time working, training, and shoeing horses so it's probably a similar cause. Every time I miss hearing something I wish I could hear as good as my old mare.

Horses have a kind of radar sense of hearing. Their ears are seldom still. They can detect a wide range of sounds from low frequency to high frequency. In other words they have acute hearing.

We two-legged creatures can hear about 20,000 cycles per second (cps) until we get up to about sixty years old and then it drops to about 12,000 cps. Horses hear at about 25,000 cps. Their hearing ability also declines with age, but they still have us beat. Why?

Well, they have radar ears. Their large, mobile external ears provide them with an acuity that we can only dream about. Now, my daddy could wiggle his big old ears to the amusement of his grandchildren, but most of can't. I don't think his wiggling skill helped his hearing at all. Horses had him beat.

Sixteen muscles control each horse ear. That's more muscles than I seem to have in my whole body. They can rotate their ears about 180 degrees so they pinpoint particular sounds from great distance. That's why when you are riding along trail and your horses ears pop forward and seem to focus on something you will discover that something really exists be it a deer, a bear, or a wild-eyed panting cyclist.

The weather bureau should hire horses. They can detect all kinds of natural disturbances like distant storms, high winds, and earthquakes. That's why some horseman insists their horse has a sixth sense. You could prove or disapprove this theory by using a deaf horse in a study. Might get a federal grant for that, as well.

What is really happening, however, is that the tiniest sounds are detect by those wonderful equine ears. That's why you don't have to shout at a horse. They can hear you perfectly. They may be just ignoring you. Sort of like some husbands do their wives.

This is not to say that horses do not have some mysterious other sense. After all, horses have been known to find their home in the dark. Some folks believe that horses respond to the earth's magnetic field like many other species. That may be. One thing is sure they are super sensitive.

That sensitivity was long overlooked by horse trainers. But it is clear that an intelligent horseman can speak softly to the horse and receive response. In fact, that is the best way to teach and control a horse. Tugging, pulling, twisting, and all those other actions are sure signs of a novice horseperson who is failing to use the horse's best attribute—a brilliant sense of hearing. As an example, my old mare will flat out run when she hears the simple word "git!"

So, take care, whisper to your horse, and ride on.

Horse Stuff worth Remembering

The modern horse is the result of 60 million years of natural selection. No! They were not created in seven days by God! As they evolved they were domesticated. They became the object of human desires to take nature even farther. Therefore, the species began to be managed by selective breeding to advance the horse even more. Our mare Ginger is an example. On her father's side, she is a double direct descendant of the famous Old Sorrel line of Quarter Horses. Her foal, Jazzy, shares that line with the stallion's direct decadency from the famous stallion Little Steel Dust who traces his heritage back to Poco Bueno. Therefore, a lot of our human culture and desire to improve things even more gives us a unique understanding of the horse. History shows us that the horse is a key element in a wide variety of human philosophies.

Take the Arab feller Yazid, who back in the 7th century, said, "A mare long of body, short of hair, whose spirit is unfailing … she is one of those steeds of race that stretch themselves fully in their gallop, springing and light of foot."

Dr. Edward Mayhew once observed," What is the use of this fuss about morality when the issue only involves a horse? The first and most difficult teaching of civilization concerns man's behavior to his inferiors. Make humanity gentle or reasonable toward animals, and strife or injustice between human beings would speedily terminate."

Back in less sensitive times the late comic Marty Allen quipped, "If a man works like a horse for his money, there are a lot of girls anxious to take him down the bridal path."

"Give a man a horse he can ride," James Thomson wrote, "Give a man a boat he can sail, And his rank and wealth, his strength and health, On sea nor shore shall fail."

You jumpers out there will appreciate this one from A.W. Hare. "Half the failures in life arise from pulling in one's horse as he is leaping."

In the Talmud it is written, "The burden is equal to the horse's strength."

Then there is Sir Alec Issigonis' comment, "A camel is a horse designed by a committee."

Blaise Pascal once noted, "Animals do not admire each other. A horse does not admire its companbion."

Noting our human weakness to run off half-cocked, Thomas Fuller once said, "A man in passion rides a horse that runs away with him."

In a similar vein Robert Collier wrote, "One might as well ride two horses moving in different directions, as to try to maintain in equal force two opposing or contradictory sets of desires."

The great poet Jelaluddin Rumi said, "Don't be the rider who gallops all night and never sees the horse beneath him."

Some folks think Bill Shakespeare said this, but it was Ben Franklin who said, "For want of a nail, the shoe was lost; for want of a shoe, the horse was lost; for want of a horse, the rider was lost." And finally, Franklin wrote in his Poor Richard's Almanack, "If you ride a horse, sit close and tight, if you ride a man sit easy and light."

So there. Check your cinch and ride on.

Horse Thieves

Where I come from the history of horse thieves is a less than desirable part of our past. Horse transportation was so important in the vast reaches of the west that to steal a horse was tantamount killing the rider. One would think that was all in the past but not so, I was reminded of this while reading an article a few weeks ago. Hanging a person from a tree limb may be outdated but horse theft is not.

Imagine waking up one morning, putting on your clothes, walking out to the barn to feed your four-legged family. You notice the open door, the open gate and the tire tracks. Your horse is missing. What do you do now? The truth is stolen horses are not very high on the list of criminal complains filed with law enforcement.

Stolen Horse International (SHI) estimates 40,000 to 50,000 horses in the US are missing or become victims of theft in one form or another each year. Even if you have not heard of horse theft before, don't think it doesn't happen. No matter what the breed or discipline of horse you enjoy, theft can happen to you.

In most western states the use of branding is essential to prevent theft and most such states have official brand inspectors with police powers. In Colorado, for instance, if you want to move a horse more than 75 miles, you better have all the proper documentation or you could end up in the hoosegow.

In the east, things are different. However, you can still brand your horse and SHI will help you develop a brand to register the horse with the appropriate state agency. The newest effort to identify horses, however, is the microchip. Implanted in the spot on the neck where you give your horse regular shots, it is read by a scanner. It is an easy and inexpensive way to establish positive identification (ID). Oh, sure you can have registration and coggins papers that tell what color the horse is and what markings are on it, but that is not enough for ID.

One way to help event horse theft is to make it difficult for the thief. Walk around the place and look at with a thief's eyes. The fact is stealing horses is easy. Nearly every place invites a thief to steal your horse, your tack, and your truck, whatever. Here are some hints that might help slow down or slop a thief.

Don't keep halters and lead ropes hanging where anyone can get to them. There is no need to give the thief the tools to steal your horse. Install security lights. Dusk to dawn and motion censor lights may not stop a determined thief but it will slow them down. Photograph your horse from all angles and in both winter and summer. Keep a file of all horse related information. Keep a barking dog, or a barking peacock. Pay attention to service vehicles in your area. Lock up tack. If you contact SHI at www.netposse.com they can provide you with microchips and other equipment as well as signs that warn thieves that your horse are permanently identified and registered. In other words, be proactive, check your barn, lock things up, and ride on.

Lead on Horse

In the past, I have made light of miniature horses. However, I recently got my comeuppance. Miniature horses are being used as guide animals. That's right—guide animals.

Now, I knew horses are natural guide animals. They have been guiding humans for centuries. I knew that in the old times, a cowboy might be injured or lost and his horse would take him home. They possess a natural guide instinct.

When another horse goes blind in a herd, a sighted horse accepts responsibility for the welfare of the blind horse and guides it with the herd. With humans, many blind people ride horses in equestrian competitions. Some blind people ride alone on trails for many miles, completely relying on the horse to guide them safely to their destination. Through history, Cavalry horses have been known to guide their injured rider to safety. There are several characteristics of horses that make them suitable to guide the blind.

1. Miniature Horse can live to be more than 50 years old, with the average lifespan being 30–40 years. According to guide dog trainers, guide dogs have a useful life between 8–12 years.

2. Training a guide dog can cost up to $60,000 and there are more than 1.3 million legally blind people in the USA, yet only 7,000 guide animal users. Therefore, a Guide Horse could be more cost-effective and ensure that more blind people receive a guide animal.

3. Many guide dog users report problems getting access to public places because their dog is perceived as a pet. Most people do not associate a horse as a pet, and Guide Horse users report that they are immediately recognized as a working service animal.

4. Trained horses are extremely calm in chaotic situations. Cavalry horses have proven that horses can remain calm even in the extreme heat of battle. Police horses are an excellent example of well trained horses that deal with stressful situations. Guide Horses undergo the same systematic desensitization training that is given to riot-control horses.

5. Horses possess phenomenal memories. A horse will naturally remember a dangerous situation decades after the occurrence.

6. Because horses have eyes on the sides of their heads, they have a very wide range of vision, with a range of nearly 350 degrees. Horses are the only guide animals capable of independent eye movement and they can track potential danger with each eye. Horses can see clearly in almost total darkness.

7. Trained horses are very focused on their work and are not easily distracted. Horses are not addicted to human attention and normally do not get excited when petted or groomed.

8. Naturally safety oriented, horses are constantly on the lookout for danger. All horses have a natural propensity to guide their master along the safest most efficient route, and demonstrate excellent judgment in obstacle avoidance training.

9. Hearty and robust, a properly conditioned Guide Horse can easily travel many miles in a single outing.

10. Guide Horses are very clean and can be housebroken. Horses do not get fleas and only shed twice per year. Horses are not addicted to human affection and will stand quietly when on duty.

Who trains these horses? Well, training any guide animal requires many years of full-time training experience. Because blind people entrust their lives to their horses, only professional horse trainers with at least ten years of full-time riding and horse training experience should attempt guide training.

So there! No more cracks about miniature horses from me. I'm checking my cinch and riding on.

Not All Cowboys and Cowgirls Are in the West

Rising primeval mists dissipated to reveal the red and gold of turning leaves among the green-blanketed Smoky Mountains as more than fifty foundation Quarter Horses, owners and exhibitors from nearly a dozen states gather in Harriman, Tennessee, for the East of the Mississippi Regional National Foundation Quarter Horse Association (NFQHA) Sanctioned Show.

I got out of my old pick-em-up truck and looked around. I thought the gods of the west had vomited cowboys all over the place. Hats, chaps, boots and spurs were everywhere providing evidence that not all cowboys live west of the Mississippi.

NFQHA members from Georgia, Alabama, Maryland, Virginia, Texas, Mississippi, Louisiana, Florida, West Virginia, Indiana, North and South Carolina were gathered for the "big" show. Like the film statement in Field of Dreams, "if you build it people will come," it was clear that if you organize a good equine event people will come.

All of the activity evolved from a quiet beginning for the National Foundation Quarter Horse Association over ten years ago. Established to reclaim the uniqueness of the foundation Quarter Horse the organization focuses on great minds, athleticism and cow sense in the horse.

They were the first organization to promote "no glitz, no glitter" in their shows; the first to introduce the In-Hand Trail classes for yearlings and two year olds; the first to offer versatility competition, a class now adopted by the American Quarter Horse Association. NFQHA became the first to disallow excessive silver in competition, the first to disallow excessive shaving of ear, nose and eye hair, the first to disallow the unhealthy practice of blacking hooves, the first to establish non-pro classes so folks do not have to compete against professional trainers. They were first to disqualify horses with unnatural gaits and posture (peanut rolling). And that, as Jack Webb of the old television show Dragnet used to say, "Is the facts, ma'am."

Dropped in among these folks, I was at once amused, impressed and encouraged by the genuine care shared by these foundation folks. I was reminded of a time long ago when I joined other volunteers to help work cattle on champion steer roper Shoat Webster's place near Lenapah, Oklahoma. No strangers, just folks you have not met before gathered to share in a common task. Each night after a raucous and talkative supper at the Cracker Barrel Restaurant, I went to the Holiday Inn Express to sleep with the pictures of Quarter Horses playing in my head.

The whole affair left a indelible imprint on my psyche. I came home with an added respect for fine versatile horses in a day when specialized horses are being bred and developed. Good horses can do whatever they are called upon to do. That's the key. For all those horses and their owners I say, ride on.

Nothing's Free

I stopped by the feed store to pick up feed for our horses and dog. While I was chatting with Sandy, the cashier, a couple entered the store. The store offers facilities for folks to stable and care for their horses. The female partner of the couple had just contracted to keep her horse there a few days before. The horse had been offered to her on a "free lease" and the lessor was due to arrive in an hour so with a contract. The lessee had some questions about whether she should enter into the contract or not, although the horse had already been delivered.

Sandy nodded toward me and said, "Here's the man to ask. Let him take a look at the horse."

The woman looked at me with questions dancing in her eyes.

Sandy said, "He's an old horseman and trainer."

The woman questions stopped dancing in her eyes and were replaced by a look of radiant joy.

"Would you come and look at him?" she asked.

I looked at Sandy and she grinned. Knowing my kind nature, she had trapped me. I almost said to the woman, "I usually get paid for this kind of work." But, I didn't. She looked frantic.

We walked out to the paddock to look at her maybe horse. He was a rangy Thoroughbred who anxiously walked the fence. He was already haltered and she handed me a lead rope. I opened the gate to enter the paddock and she said, "You won't be able to catch him without a bucket with feed."

I acknowledge her advice and asked if we might try something different. She smiled and said, "Sure."

I entered the paddock and the bay moved down the fence away from me. She started to follow me into the paddock and I ask her to wait outside while I tried something. She closed the gate and stood watching as I walked to the center of the paddock, and stood there with the lead rope in hand. I said nothing. The horse stopped walking the fence line and looked at me. Then, as he quietly ambled over to where I stood I snapped the lead onto his halter, I head her say, "Man, you're good."

41

I looked the horse over and noted he had a bell boot on one front foot and the other front hoof was grown out in a hideous reflection of what was obviously the result of founder.

"Isn't he a great horse?" she asked with a hint of disappointment in her voice as I led him out of the paddock. "What do you think?"

Wrong question to ask an old codger like me. I told her what I thought: founder, vet and farrier bills, the need for some serious ground training, and a winter's feed and care. My advice: Just say no because nothing is ever free. Then, I told her what I really thought. "This horse person saw you coming, ma'am. She just wants you to pay the bills until she is ready to take the horse back."

She thanked me and said she would say, "No," although she obviously had fallen in love with the horse.

My job was done. Free advice for those seeking a free lease. Be very careful, check your cinch and ride on.

Old Beans and a Day at the Track

Old Beans Taylor is a devoted churchman with one little flaw. He loves to sneak away to the racetrack. One day he was there betting on the ponies and nearly losing his shirt when he noticed this priest who stepped out onto the track and blessed one of the horses lining up for the 4th race.

Beans checked his racing form and noticed that this horse was a long shot—a very long shot and he won the race. Beans was aghast. The horse, according to his past record, did not have a chance and yet he won. Therefore, Beans kept a close eye on the priest as the next race was about to start. Sure enough, the priest step out onto the track as the fifth racehorses lined up, and blessed one of the horses. Beans didn't waver. He made a beeline for the window and placed a small bet on the horse. Again, even though it was another long shot, the horse the priest blessed won the race. Beans collected his winnings and eagerly waited to see which horse the priest blessed for the sixth race. The priest showed up again and blessed a horse. Beans bet on it, and it won! He was beside himself. As the day went on, the priest continued blessing one of the horses in every race and that horse always came in first.

Beans was pulling in some serious money and by the last race, he knew his wildest dreams were going to come true. He made a quick stop at the ATM, withdrew all the money he had in the bank and waited for the priest to bestow his blessing.

Sure enough, just before the last race the priest came onto the track did a major blessing. He blessed the forehead, eyes, ears and hooves of one of the horses. "This is it," Beans said to himself as he went to the window to bet every cent he had. Then he sat smiling in the stands as the race began and the smile faded as the horse came in dead last.

Old Beans was beside himself. He angrily made his way to the track and when he found the priest, he demanded, "What happened, Father? All day you blessed horses and they won. The last race, you blessed a horse and he lost. Now I've lost my life's savings, thanks to you!"

The priest looked at him with a calm demeanor and pastorally said, "That's the problem with you Protestants … you can't tell the difference between a simple blessing and Last Rites."

Origin of the Horse

Those of us who are fascinated with history, archeology, anthropology and mythology are always reading about the things we love. Therefore, I have been delving into the origins of the horse. Just in case some of neophytes out there think the horse is a late comer to the world I have come to bear witness to ancient times.

It is probable, the scholars tell us, that the first horse (paleohippus) existed about fifty three million years ago. Now that is longer than my farrier Tom and I have been around, although some may argue that point. About thirteen million years later eohippis emerged in what are now the high plains of western Kansas and eastern Colorado. He stood about a foot high and looked like an odd dog. His teeth had not evolved so he had eat soft foods, but he had a tail to fight the flies, a kind of furry coat, and a long face filled with forty-four teeth, four toes on the front feet and three on the back feet. Now that would be farrier's nightmare.

About thirty million years ago, his successor emerged. Folks who do those kinds of things named it mesohippus. Now, he was a little more like we think a horse should be. About the size of a collie or a fox, he was some twenty-four inches at the withers and now he had three toes on each foot and they still had a kind of pad on their toes but they were beginning to look more like hoofs. Twelve million years later merychippus appeared.

Now this forty-inch high hay burner was a little prettier than his predecessors were. He had bristly mane and protective bone bars behind his eye sockets. What was really different was his teeth they had developed so they continued to grow from the socket as they worn down eating the short grass on the prairie. He still had three toes but they were not going to last long. Six million years later, they would have only one toe. They call these one toed creatures pliohippus. He looked like the modern horse except he was smaller than the average horse today.

Finally, about two million years ago the horse as we know it emerged. They named it equus. It had all the best features of its ancestors. Time took care of that. And that is how we got "Old Dobbin," or whatever you call your horse. Oh, and by the way, although they seemed to have originated in North America for some reason they migrated to Asia over a large land mass that connected the two continents and, thereby, disappeared from our continent. They reappeared with the Spanish invasion.

So, that's the story. Clean your saddle, wash the blanket, and ride on.

Rags and Beans Address the Killer Issue

I knew it was just a matter of time. When I saw Old Beans' pick-em-up truck come slip sliding to a stop in my driveway I figured he and Rags were hot about something. I started pouring them a cup of coffee before they even hit the door.

Rags threw his John Deere gimme cap across the room and flopped down in a kitchen chair. Beans stood by the table, reached down for his mug of coffee and growled.

"Now they've done it. The cat's out of the bag."

I sat down at the table, sipped my coffee, and looked up at him.

"Who are they and what does cat's out of the bag mean?"

He looked at me like I was the village idiot.

"That's an old saying," he said.

"Must be," I said. "Since you're saying it."

This time he just gave me the look my mama gave me when I went too far.

Rags intercepted his next growl and said, "Congress has passed a law banning the slaughter of horses for human consumption, several states have also passed laws like that and the Supreme Court won't consider overturning them."

"Know what that means," Beans snorted. "We are going to have old, cripple, homeless horses wandering the streets looking for a place to lay down and die. Homeless horses. Probably be on the street corners begging, the next thing you know. Thousands of them. Standing on street corners."

Rags and I looked at him with pity in our eyes.

"That's some imagination you got there, old hoss," Rags said.

"And you old boys know all of this because?" I asked rhetorically.

"Studies," Rags said. "The Animal Welfare Council says the cost of maintaining unwanted horses is going to be around $220 million per year."

"And they got friends who agree with them," Beans added. "The American Association of Equine Practitioners, The American Quarter Horse Association, even circuses and the rodeo folks."

"It is a problem," I said quietly hoping Beans would settle down before he busted that blood vessel I saw pounded in his forehead.

Rags looked around the kitchen before asking, "No doughnuts?"

"Nope."

"Well," he said. "They are figuring there will be 60,000 to 90,000 unwanted horses and no place to put them."

"And the bottom is falling out of the horse market," Beans snorted. "You can't even give away a grade animal anymore. Registered stock is not much better."

"You know where they're taking the slaughter animals?" Rags asked. "Mexico and Canada. They still butcher then for the Europeans and Japanese to eat."

"Now they're talking about passing a law to keep horse folk from trucking them across the border to slaughter houses," Old Beans muttered. "Where will it end?"

"We only had three plants in the U.S. before they shut them down," Rags said. "The Mexicans have eight regular ones to saying nothing about the mom and pop independents."

"At least the Canadians have strict rules like the U.S.D.A. had for our slaughter houses," Beans said.

"I agree it is a problem," I said, stating the obvious.

"Damn right," Beans snarled. "String them up, I say."

"Who?" I asked.

"Ignorant animal rights people," Beans snapped. "Don't know a biscuit from a road apple."

"Think of it, Vern," Rags ignored him. "Maybe a 100,000 horses a year with no one to care for them."

"What's going to happen?" Beans asked. "And don't you tell us to check our cinch and ride on or I'll whack you one."

"I don't know," I said. "I wish I did."

"Well," Rags said. "We got to go. Thanks for listening."

"Your welcome."

"Just don't say it," Beans added.

"What?"

"Check your cinch and ride on," he said, slapped himself on the forehead and muttered something unintelligible that sounded something like horse apples, as they left, got into their old pick-em-truck and drove away in a cloud of dust.

Spirituality and Horses

There is an eastern form of spirituality called Reiki Kanji. It involves healing and self-care. One of the ways we can do that is through our relationship with horses. The question then becomes "How?"

I suggest that we come to horses to re-member the scattered stories that lie buried in forgotten caves. Historians are aware that throughout the ages, folks entered the earth's womb, the deepest caves, to commune in the darkness with the Spirit that unites us all. Night after night, we kept going inside of ourselves developing an intimate relationship with the Great Mystery and through that process of dream upon dream, we became empowered to be co-creators of the world in which we live. So, where do horses come into all this?

Some the earliest human art discovered on the walls of caves portray horses. In Spanish, the ancient root word for "caballo" meaning horse is "cava" or cave. It seems to me that beyond the form we often idealize, the horse's inner nature has the power to transform us from the inside out. Horses are powerful medicine move us from the light to the shadows and back again, repeatedly.

Anyone who has ever felt moved to talk to his or her horse and felt a kind of silent understanding, knows what I am getting at. K.F. Hepfling in his book **What Horses Reveal** says the horse is "always met only in his extremes. It is important to know and assimilate this knowledge before coming together with horses, because, whoever does not realize that he is not only symbolically with a snake when he stands before a horse, will, sooner or later, get his soul 'bitten'."

Culturally, we fear shadows, darkness and evasiveness. Therefore, we try to control and dominate that fear. We are taught to escape into transcendent reality and idealism because it seems safer then trusting in the wisdom of our bodies and the changing nature of the earth.

The old form Reiki Kanji is described as a shaman standing on the earth with his arms raised to the sky from which comes lifesaving energy like rain falling from the heavens bringing Light, Love and Wisdom. The shaman is the channel bridging heaven and earth helping us to be inspirited. That is, we are moved to allow ourselves to experience the sacred through the familiar, matter, mother, bodies, horses, the mud on our skin, the bark of a tree, the smell of pine needles.

Horses are guides into sacredness. And whether we know it or not that is why horses pull us into their lives. Thank God for horses.

The Dorrance Legacy

Most every sensible horse trainer owes a lot of what they do to Tom Dorrance. I was reminded of this while visiting in Joseph, Oregon. That's where he lived and folks there are right proud of him. They even have a street named for him.

With all the "Natural Horsemanship" trainers around selling books, tapes and holding clinics, it is good to remember that they probably got most of their ideas from Tom Dorrance.

There is a story about a day when Dorrance was visiting a ranch where they were branding calves. The rancher offered his horse to Dorrance so he could rope a few calves. Dorrance politely declined.

"No," he said. "I don't want to take your horse." Then, he pointed to a couple of horses in a nearby pasture and asked, "What are those horses over there?"

They're not broke, was the reply.

Whereupon, Dorrance, asked, "Would it be all right if I rode one of them?"

Puzzled, they said, sure. The story goes that he drove away to the other pasture and returned in about thirty minutes on horseback. There were cows and calves milling around, bawling, as they are want to do during a branding. Cowboys on horses were darting into the herd, swinging their ropes, and dragging out calves. The branding fire roared. Cowboys wrestled down calves. Others carried hot branding irons in and out of the chaos. And Dorrance rode into this melee on an unbroken horse and proceeded to rope one calf after another and drag it to the fire.

His legacy, however, was more than his natural ability to relate to horses. He was, his friends say, quiet and self-effacing without any desire to be famous or rich. And unlike so many "natural horsemanship" trainers today, he eschewed self-promotion. In the conventional sense, he had no ego requiring him to seek fame. He was, however, a natural genius with horses so people sought him out. He seemed to possess mysterious powers when it came to relating to horses.

Tom Dorrance died in June, 2003. However, he lives on in the revolutionary steps taken in natural horsemanship to the benefit of horses and riders everywhere.

So, Tom, we hope the horses in the great beyond provide you with a challenge and joy.

The Female of the Species

I read an article in Western Horseman about a rancher on a big spread in Utah who believes as I do and that is always nice. Like me, he has an affinity for mares. Although I have ridden geldings and stallions in my time, I have always felt that mares displayed more intelligence and staying power than their male counterparts did.

So, I put my mind to working on the reasons for this and came up with an answer. I did so by considering my experience with mares, but primarily I just looked around at all the female human beans I have known.

My mother worked from daylight until long into the night. Not only did she bear five and raise five children, physical labor never scared her. One winter while my daddy was sick in bed for an extended length of time, she and I, neither of us weighing more than a hundred pounds milked forty cows morning and night and shoveled silage to feed them everyday for many weeks. Then I went to school and she worked all day at caring for daddy and doing her usual household chores.

Her mother, Grandma Amrine, did the same with ten children. My daddy's mother, Grandma Schmid had twelve, lived on a farm and raised them without any going to prison and she was never sent to the madhouse. Tough ladies. And yet, they are not unusual. The female of every species has that kind of strength and courage including Miss Susan.

We only have two daughters (who show those tough traits) but Miss Susan has never balked at hard work. Additionally she has willingly followed me across many states (Kansas, Colorado, Missouri, Pennsylvania, Delaware and Maryland) as I pursued my career and dreamed dreams.

Therefore, I have reached the conclusion that the female of species if tougher and more courageous than the males. Oh, and they are smarter, too. Intelligence radiates from them. No wonder some horsemen prefer mares. They are a reflection of all that is good in every species, including our own. So, there it is. One man's opinion. Now, check your cinch and ride on.

The Horse Trailer Incident

It all started while I was sick in bed during the Maryland Horse Expo at Timonium, Maryland. Because of my illness, Miss Susan and our eldest daughter, Susanna, went to the event without me. They had a purpose. Check out the horse trailers.

At thirty-five years and counting, our old two-horse unit was showing its age. It was clearly time to get a new one. My feverish state was interrupted by a report on a regular ten minute basis as the two went from dealer to dealer, horse trailer to horse trailer, shopping. The first thing they noted was that many of the dealers ignored them. Miss Susan later observed that it was probably because they were women. Then, they encountered a very nice young man, a manufacturer's rep, who not only visited with them but took the time to show them what he had at the show.

Miss Susan explained that we wanted a three-horse slant load. He showed her the possibilities. The phone calls kept coming in and my response to each call was the same. "Just buy it and let me sleep."

They did not buy a trailer. They came home with an armload of brochures, prices and a warm feeling about the makers of Bee Trailers down in Georgia and the guy who treated them with respect.

Weeks passed and one day Miss Susan said, "You know there is another show at Harrisburg, Pennsylvania. Why don't you go on line and see if they are going to be there. That way you could see what we saw."

I did. They were scheduled to be there. Therefore, we went. Sure enough, the pleasant young man was there with his trailers. I asked him to show his wares, keeping in mind, I did not want anything fancy and I did not want to spend any money. He smiled and showed us a combo, three-horse slant load, gooseneck with dressing room. The show price was a thousand dollars less than suggested retail and we bought it.

In the process of finalizing the deal, I mentioned how other trailer reps in Maryland had treated Miss Susan and our daughter. He laughed and told us a story.

It seems he was at a show in Ohio when two women began looking at his trailers. He said they looked like bag ladies and he did not hold out much hope of selling them anything, but he patiently showed them what he had. Finally, they settled on a $50,000 living quarters horse trailer, sat down and one of the women wrote him a check for the full amount. It seems she was a gynecologist and the other woman was her friend. The episode taught him a lesson. You can never tell by the way that a person is dressed what their possibilities are. As an old country song goes, "There's lumps in their clothes, got to look for those."

Bottom line, we got us a new trailer from a good manufacturer, lifetime warranty on the floor, and left the place with a great feeling. Then the adventure really started.

Four weeks after purchase, they called to say our trailer was at the lot, in Virginia. Miss Susan, our friend Keith, a Quarter Horse owner and trainer, and I took a two-hour trip to pick up a new gooseneck three-horse slant trailer.

We signed all the papers, hooked it up and as we were leaving the lot I rubbed one of the trailer's fenders against the back bumper of one of the workers pick-em-up trucks. No damage, just a slight black mark on the trailer fender. As I turned to enter the highway, I narrowly missed a mailbox. Keith and Miss Susan were hooting, hollering, and laughing at my antics.

I explained that it had been a long time since I pulled a gooseneck trailer. I promised that it would all be fine by the time we made the two-hour trip home. They were not convinced.

Miss Susan sat in the back seat of the extended cab of our pick-em-up truck and offered the usual back seat directives. Keith just sat and laughed in his quiet way, but I noticed he had a good grip on the handhold in front of the shotgun seat. To this day his fingerprints remain as reminders.

She kept warning me of dangers; he kept offering me good sound advice. Therefore, for two hours I was trapped in the cab of my pick-em-up truck with wisdom and experience. I was also the butt of their running jokes.

One such joke was that I hit the mailbox and a man standing beside it and the mailbox and man were hooked onto the back of trailer and he was waving and shouting for me to stop.

The other joke Miss Susan developed was this: We need a sign on the front of the trailer declaring, "Old man driving pick-em-up truck pulling a trailer—get out of the way."

I realized I deserved their razzing when after driving about 20 miles; I looked down and saw the truck was in third gear instead of drive. Like a fool, I mentioned the mistake. Keith just looked disappointed and gripped the handhold a little tighter. I think I heard Miss Susan mutter something about old age and stupidity being partners. Finally, shifting into drive we hit the crowded interstate highway. Both passengers got very quiet. Upon arrival home, we parked the trailer and only then did someone mention that while others tow their trailers in the slow lane on the interstate, I tow mine in the fast lane.

Therefore, if you meet a Chevy Silverado pulling a gooseneck horse trailer down the road remember the slogan: "Old man driving pick-em-up truck pulling a trailer—get out of the way."

Who Would Have Thunk It?

Who would have thunk it? That stuff we do to our horses, just because we care for them has evolved into a "profession." It's called "equine massage."

Like a lot of other things, clinicians and colt starters for example, some of us should have caught on years ago and became pioneers of the profession. I'm not putting it down, I am just frustrated because I never thought about it a way to care for horses and earn money at the same time.

Now, Miss Susan, I, and our daughters have all engaged in massage. We like it. It feels good and it gets rid of a lot knots and such in our muscles, tendons, and ligaments. The difference is you don't give the horse herbal tea and a soft robe to wear while waiting your turn and you don't ask the horse to lie on its back, or stomach while the massage is taking place. The benefits, however, are the same.

Objectives include such simple things as "feeling good." In a more serious vein, the massage may help heal and injury, improve circulation and relieve tension. These can result from any number of things like training, hard work like cutting or jumping, reining and rodeo timed events.

A lot of us have rubbed our horses just behind their ears below the mane. They seem to enjoy it, so we do it. However, it also a key point for massage therapy. Along the withers and down the front shoulders is also a significant area, as is the girth area. Like you and I, the hips are loaded with pressure points that relieve a lot of pressure and tension.

There are some indications that your horse could use a little tender care like a massage. They include loss of impulsion or suppleness, reduced range of motion, head tossing and shaking, sore back, bracing against or avoiding a bit, uneven muscular development, difficulty coordinating, refusing or resisting leads, girthing problems, unwillingness or inability to walk up or down inclines, poor disposition or poor eating and resting habits. Maybe the old pony is just having an off day. All can benefit from a good massage.

The key is to rub the areas with a thin glove on you hand. When you feel warmth through the glove, stop rubbing that area and move on. You might also consider stretching just like a runner or athlete stretches before taking off. Stand in front of the horse reach down, grasp it gently behind the knee, and pull the leg forward. You can do this on all four legs. If the horse tries to kill your farrier when he picks up a leg, you may want to consult a professional equine massage therapist.

After more than sixty years around horses and watching demonstrations by some "pros," these are just a few basics. They can really help your horse live a better life and he or she will love you for it. So check your cinch, rub the old pony down and ride on.

Cowboys and Other Critters

A Nebraska Cowboy Christmas

We all have a Christmas times that stand out in our memory. One of mine occurred fifty years ago on the snow burdened cold high plains of Nebraska.

My best friend in the army was Chuck Wiggins. We served together in the 19th Military Police Command at Fort Carson, Colorado. A CID (Criminal Investigation Department) unit, it was independent of the Army division assigned to the post. We were responsible for criminal investigation, policing, gate security, town patrols and the stockade. Chuck and I were stockade guards who took prisoners on work details around the post and delivered prisoners into the hands of the FBI on occasion. We were also the only two cowboy types in the unit. I was a wannabe bronc rider. He was a rancher's son who loved to rope.

On Christmas Eve as we studied what to do with our holiday leave time Chuck had the answer. We would leave right after work, go to the Wiggin's ranch for Christmas, and surprise his family. So, on Christmas Eve we got in his yellow Buick convertible with the top up for a change and headed north and west out of Colorado, across the corner of into the high rolling plains of Nebraska.

It was a long night but in the early morning hours we came to a tiny snow filled rutted road off the back country highway we had been traveling. Chuck stopped the car and we sat looking up the tracks in the snow that seemed to lead to nowhere. He was smiling. He was home for Christmas.

Then we began to drive up those ruts into the long white darkness. Within a couple of miles, the Buick spun out and refused to move. Church said, "No problem" and walked off into the night. I sat there wondering if I would freeze to death. After an hour or so, a tractor appeared in the darkness with two grinning Wiggins boys aboard. Chuck's younger brother hooked a chain to the front of the Buick and pulled us on into the Wiggins homestead.

We fell into beds and slept a short sleep. The smell of breakfast cooking and the chatter of young girls awakened me while it was still dark. I rolled out bed, pulled on my jeans, flannel shirt and boots, and clomped down the stairs. There was Chuck, his brother, dad, mother and sisters all bright eyed and cheery. As I entered the room, a chorus of voices shouted "Merry Christmas." We ate a quick breakfast of beef sausage, eggs, hotcakes, and coffee and headed to the barn.

With a team of horses pulling a wagon, we drove across the prairie scattering hay for herds of milling Hereford cattle. When finished we headed into the house. It was time to open presents.

I don't know where they found the after shave they wrapped in bright paper and topped with a bow. Nevertheless, I shall never forget that Christmas gift, or that day.

We spent part of the day riding green broke horses in a round pen and then Chuck and I saddled up and headed across the icy prairie. There was a girl on a neighboring ranch he wanted to see. There were few fences, but when we came to one Chuck dismounted, took his fencing tool out of his saddlebag and pulled the staples. We held down the barbed wire and led the horses across and he hammered in the staples. After a short howdy and a Merry Christmas at the other ranch we headed back across that vast prairie to the Wiggins place.

That Christmas is one I shall never forget. The friendliness, the good cheer, the gift, the love of a family toward a stranger are things that resonate in memory. May all your Christmases sing their way into your heart for all time.

An Old Rancher's Advice

I am not sure where I get a lot of this stuff, but it just keeps coming my way in letters and stories and on the internet. Folks send me things they think I can use, or that it will give me a chuckle. This collection of an old rancher's advice makes sense.

Your fences need to be horse-high, pig-tight and bull-strong.

Keep skunks and bankers and lawyers at a distance.

Life is simpler when you plow around a stump.

A bumblebee is considerably faster than a John Deere tractor.

Words that soak into your ears are whispered … not yelled. Meanness don't jes' happen overnight.

Forgive your enemies. It messes up their heads.

Do not corner something that you know is meaner than you are.

It don't take a very big person to carry a grudge.

You cannot unsay a cruel word.

Every trail has a few puddles.

When you wallow with pigs, expect to get dirty.

The best sermons are lived, not preached.

Most of the stuff people worry about ain't never gonna happen anyway.

Don't judge folks by their relatives.

Remember that silence is sometimes the best answer.

Live a good, honorable life. Then when you get older and think back, you'll enjoy it a second time.

Don't interfere with somethin' that ain't botherin' you none.

Timing has a lot to do with the outcome of a rain dance.

If you find yourself in a hole, the first thing to do is stop digging.

Sometimes you get, and sometimes you get got.

The biggest troublemaker you'll probably ever have to deal with, watches you from the mirror every morning. Always drink upstream from the herd.

Good judgment comes from experience, and a lot of that comes from bad judgment.

Letting the cat out of the bag is a whole lot easier than putting it back in.

If you get to thinking you're a person of some influence, try ordering somebody else's dog around.

Live simply. Love generously. Care deeply. Speak kindly. Leave the rest to God.

Assault and Battery

Some rancher friends in southwest Colorado raise Quarter Horses and to increase their income they run a stable that rents horses for dudes to ride on an hourly or daily basis. They also lead fishing and hunting pack trips into the San Juan Mountains. Rick, the husband of the team, is a former rodeo cowboy. He has moved from riding rough stock to roping. Therefore, there is always a rope on his saddle.

A few years ago, he took a hunting camp into the mountains where he has a federal permit to establish such a camp for hunting purposes. He took along some help in the shape of a young wrangler and also a big old boy he had known for many years to establish base camp before bringing in the hunters. When they arrived at their campsite beside a small mountain stream, they discovered some other folks camped on the other side of the stream. They were settling in and getting ready to go hunting the next morning.

Not being the shy and reserved type, Rick informed them they were in violation of federal law and that he had the proper permit for using this particular site. Whereupon, the folks ensconced on his campsite got a bit abusive linguistically. Rick explained it to them again and they said they had paid good money to be there. Rick knew immediately what had happened. Someone had charged them a stiff fee to use the area disregarding requirements for a permit.

Well, the cowboy in Rick came to the surface, according to the young wrangler who was keeping out of the debate. Rick told them to pack up and "Git." One of the interlopers moved aggressively toward Rick's helper, I'll call "Big'Un." When the aggressive feller got too close Big'Un smacked him in the nose and sent him sprawling with a broken proboscis. Another feller moved in on the fight and Rick, still mounted, roped him and dragged him a ways. The wrangler remained with the stock not seeking to involve himself in melee. It seems the interlopers then packed up and left the scene. Rick's crew set up the base camp and rode home.

When they reached the ranch, the sheriff's department was waiting for them with warrants for assault and battery. They informed Rick that the federal agencies had been notified about the permit violation, but the hunters insisted on pressing charges against Rick and Big'Un. Rick said he understood why Big'Un should be arrested for assault and battery, but he was perplexed by the idea that roping and dragging was a chargeable offense.

Epilogue: Faced with federal charges the interlopers chose to vacate the area and the charges against Rick and Big'Un were quietly dropped. Nuff said.

Aunt Rosie's Breakfasts

When I was fifteen years of age, I quit high school for the second time. The first time the president of the school board gave me a job in his lumberyard. I spent months unloading boxcars of lumber. That job got me interested in trying high school again. However, as usual, after a few months I was disillusioned and quit again. That's when Uncle John came to the rescue.

My mama's brother, Uncle John, had never wanted to be anything but a cowboy. He was the first of the immediate family to go west and get a job on a Colorado ranch. World War II came along and Uncle John went into the army and served as a surgeon's assistant. On leave, he started dating Aunt Rosie and when the war ended he came home, they got married and headed west. By the time my family moved to Colorado he and Rosie had three children and were ranching south of town near Ruby Mountain. When I quit high school, he told mama and daddy he would give me a job on his ranch.

I was beside myself. All I ever wanted to be was a cowboy, just like Uncle John. Now, I could pursue that dream. I was already and accomplished horseman and working the ranch seemed to fit right into the scheme of things I had planned for my life. So, I packed up my stuff and headed for the ranch.

Unfortunately, what Uncle John wanted me to do had little or nothing to do with horses and cattle. My job, day after day, week after week, month after month, was to track long handle shovel and stand in a field and direct irrigation water onto the crops or hay meadows. Did I say, day after day, week after week, month after month? The only highlight of this experience was Aunt Rosie's breakfasts.

I would wake up in the dark, dress, wash my face and stumble down to the kitchen where everyone would gather at the table. With the sound of Eddie Arnold's radio show, accompanying our breakfast Aunt Rosie would begin placing food on the table. To this day, I can conjure up the smells and my mouth will water. Sausage links, eggs, scratch biscuits and waffles with real butter and thick maple syrup, hot coffee and orange juice. After breakfast, I would pull on my rubber boots and head for the field.

Uncle John did have me help with other chores around the ranch, but I never had the experience being a "real" cowboy. But, neither of us ever brought it up. What kept me going was being able to work outdoors with Ruby Mountain as a backdrop and Aunt Rosie's breakfasts. I would go to sleep at night anticipating not the work the next day but Aunt Rosie's breakfasts.

Like my folks they are both gone now. But, fond memories remain especially those mornings when the family gathered for breakfast. Oh, by the way, the day my daddy came and got me Uncle John gave me one more job. He asked me to take a two-year-old black colt home with me to train. I did and as I look back on the ranch experience and Aunt Rosie's breakfasts I am always conscious of the fact that Uncle John taught me how to work and in the end gave me a sweet reward in the shape of that black colt.

Cowboy Cookout Menu

Appetizers
Steaks
Beans
Potato Salad
Sourdough Bread
Cole Slaw
Cobbler

Entree
Steak
Beans
Cole Slaw
Potato Salad
Sourdough Bread
Cobbler

Dessert
Steak
Beans
Sourdough Bread
Potato Salad
Cole Slaw
Cobbler

Cowboy Social Tips

1. Never take a beer to a job interview.

2. Always identify people in your yard and pasture before shooting at them.

3. Never take a cooler to church.

4. If you have to vacuum the bed, it's time to change the sheets.

5. Even if you are certain you are included in a will, it's rude to pull your goose-neck stock trailer to the funeral.

6. When decanting the wine from the box, make sure you tilt the paper cup and pour slowly so as not to 'bruise' the fruit of the wine.

7. If drinking directly from the bottle, always hold it with your hands.

8. The centerpiece for your table should never be anything prepared by a taxidermist.

9. Never allow your blue heeler to eat at the table, no matter how good his manners are.

10. While ears need to be cleaned regularly, this job should be done in private using one's own truck keys.

11. Even if you live alone, deodorant is not a waste of money.

12. Use of proper toiletries only delays bathing for a few days.

13. Dirt, saddle soap, and grease under the fingernails is a social no-no, as they tend to distract from a woman's jewelry, and alter the taste of finger foods.

14. If you take your date fishing offer to bait her hook on the first date.

15. Never say to a woman, "I've been wanting to go out with you ever since I read that stuff on the bathroom walls two years ago."

16. Refrain from talking to the characters on the movie screen. Tests have proven that they can't hear you.

17. Livestock is a poor choice for a wedding gift.

18. Kissing another man's bride at the wedding reception for more than 5 seconds could get you shot.

19. Dim your headlights for approaching vehicles, even if the gun is loaded and the deer is in sight.

20. When approaching four way stops, the vehicle with the largest tires does not always have the right of way.

21. Never tow another car using panty hose and duct tape.

22. When sending your wife down the road with a gas can, it is impolite to ask her to bring back beer too.

23. Do not lay rubber while traveling in a funeral possession.

Cowboy Wisdom

Rags Bandy comes by often to share a little cowboy wisdom. The other morning over a cup of coffee, he asked how my traveling has been. I told him I had just returned from a Schmid family reunion in Kansas where ninety Schmids turned up to party.

"That's a bunch," he said. "And if they are all like you the prospect of such a gathering is a downright scary."

I agreed and added that I considered myself the prettiest one in attendance.

"Then they shore must be an ugly clan," he commented and then added, "But, you can't judge people by their relatives."

"That is a true saying," I said.

"I got more," he said as he poured his coffee into a saucer to let it cool.

"Like what?"

"Never approach a bull from the front, a horse from the rear, or a fool from any direction."

"I like that," I said while watching him sip his coffee from the saucer.

"I got a long list," he said. "Folks just don't pay me no mind when I tell them things like behind every successful rancher is a wife who works in town."

"You got that right."

"Want to hear some more wise sayings," he asked.

"Why not," I said. "I ain't got a thing to do until Miss Susan gets home and then I have to watch her clean stalls."

"Then here goes."

"Talk slow, think quick."

"Sometimes silence is the best answer."

"Don't interfere with something that ain't bothering you none."

"It's better to be a has-been that a never-was."

"The easiest way to eat crow is while it's still warm. The colder it gets, the harder it is to swaller."

"If it don't seem like it's worth the effort, it probably ain't."

"It don't take a genius to spot a goat in a flock of sheep."

"The biggest troublemaker you'll probably ever have to deal with watches you shave his face in the mirror every morning."

"If you get to thinking you're a person of some influence, try orderin' somebody else's dog around."

"Always drink upstream from the herd."

"Generally, you ain't learning nothing when your jaws are flapping."

"If you're riding ahead of the herd, take a look back every now and then to make sure it's still there with you."

"Good judgment comes from experience, and a lot of that comes from bad judgment."

"When you give a personal lesson in meanness to a critter or to a person, don't be surprised if they learn their lesson."

"The quickest way to double your money is to fold it over and put it back into your pocket."

"You can't tell how good a man or a watermelon is 'til they get thumped."

I interrupted.

"You mean, Character shows up best when tested."

"That's right, perfesser," he said. "And never miss a good chance to shut up. And now, here's a final note of wisdom. If lawyers are disbarred and clergymen are defrocked, shouldn't it follow that cowboys would be deranged?"

I was still laughing when he got up and went out to his pick-em-truck and drove away.

Duct Tape Cowboys

I read a book written by two fellers who have a love affair with duct tape. Their number one rule is "If it ain't stuck and it's supposed to be, duct tape it."

I thought about their attitude and realized that many of their ideas fit right in with the cowboy way. To quote a great cowboy philosopher, "It may not be the right way, but it's the cowboy way."

Consider this. If you have a loose tooth fasten one end of duct tape to the tooth, wrap the other end around a saddle and spook the horse. That'll do it.

When the icy wind on the prairie causes your nose to begin to drip just stick a piece of duct tape over the holes. It will stop the dripping and if others are around you save yourself the embarrassment of dripping in front of them. And if the cold gets real bad and drops down into your chest forget grandma's mustard plaster. Duct tape a dozen mustard packets stole from a local cafe across your chest. It is a lot less messy.

The next time you are thrown off a recalcitrant horse cover your cuts and bruises with duct tape as needed to stop the bleeding. Or use it in combination with pieces of your blanket as a compress.

On long highway stretches across Nebraska or the Dakotas on your way to the next rodeo tape your steering wheel to the dashboard and the gas pedal to the floor and catch a few winks.

Caught out punching cows without your chaps? Duct tape wrapped around your britches will work just as well and you can tape the top of boots closed to keep out the burrs and centipedes.

All you bronc riders can solve the problem of being thrown by duct taping yourself to the saddle. Yee Haw!

Put a strip of duct tape on your pick-em-up truck's bumper. No words just tape. It'll speak volumes.

Saddle repairs can be made easily by just duct taping things together. If anyone ridicules you tell them it its new technology and they should get on the band-wagon.

Hat fly off at a full gallop? Fold a strip of duct tape so that both sides are sticky and place it around the inside of your hatband. Problem solved and no sissy stampede strings needed.

Got a problem with tailgaters. Duct tape a large mirror to your pick-em-truck or horse trailer's tailgate. In daytime the glare from the mirror will keep them back, at night their own headlights will confuse them as they think another car is coming at them in their own lane.

So, there you are all alone at a line camp and your sinuses start acting up. Duct tape a pan filled with water and smelly medicine to your face, set the pan on the stove and inhales the steam. While you are breaking up the sinus congestion, you get a nice facial.

Well, you get the idea. Check your cinch, repair it with duct tape and ride on.

Ranching Tales

As anyone who has ever visited Wyoming knows, they hold an annual wind festival there from January 1—December 31.

Trees lean with the wind and so do the natives. They all list as they walk like sailors trying to keep they balance on board a ship. In addition to this there is a perpetual accumulation of tumbleweeds against walls, cars, trucks, slow walking folks, and fences. Victims of this natural western occurrence include everyone but none suffers as much ranchers whose fences are in constant peril from this natural predator. The seemingly harmless tumbleweeds pile up to such an extent that they can bring down fences.

A rancher of some renown had fought this seemingly loosing battle against this enemy year after year. One day he came up with a unique solution. Instead of going out with his hired hands to pick up the tumbleweeds every year, he devised a method of burning them. It worked.

His inventive approach burned the tumbleweeds on the spot and his miles long fence line is tumbleweed free. He was very proud of himself until he checked the miles of fence line he had cleared and discovered that not only had the tumbleweeds burned so did his fence posts. Now he is at work building fence and trying to think of another way to control tumbleweeds in a part of the west where wind and weeds are historic partners.

In another part of the country, Kansas to be exact, a horse rancher had put in the new white vinyl fencing around his pastures, paddocks and the like. You don't have to paint them and if a horse breaks a vinyl board the company will replace it. The feller was really happy with this addition to the ranch.

When fall came, he went out to burn off the pasture which is a traditional way of getting rid of weeds and having good grass come up in the spring. You guessed it. When he finished the pasture was nice but the fire had melted down his fence.

Ranching is a hard life, so tighten your cinch and ride on.

Rocks and Sand

An old cowboy listened to the bunkhouse men discussing matters of life. He left the room and came back with a gallon Mason jar and bucket full of rocks. Saying nothing he put the jar on the table and proceeded to fill it with rocks about 2" in diameter. He then asked the puzzled men if the jar was full?

They all agreed that it was.

So the old timer got some pebbles out of the bucket and poured them into the jar. He shook the jar lightly and the pebbles rolled into the open areas between the rocks. He then asked the watchful cowboys again if the jar was full. They laughed and agreed it was.

The old cowboy lifted the bucket and poured sand out of it into the jar. Of course, the sand filled up everything else.

Now," said the old cowboy, "This is like your life. The rocks are the important things—your family, your saddle pal, your health, your family—anything that is so important to you that if it were lost, you would be nearly destroyed. The pebbles are the other things that matter like your job, your horse, your old pick-em-up-truck. The sand is everything else. The small stuff."

"If you put the sand into the jar first, there is no room for the pebbles or the rocks. The same goes for your life. If you spend all your energy and time on the small stuff, you will never have room for the things that are important to you. Pay attention to the things that are critical to your happiness.

Play with children. Get the Doc to check you out now and then. Take your sweetheart out dancing.

"There is always be time to go to work, brand cattle, ride a roundup, break a horse, have a hooray, or fix the tack.

Take care of the rocks first—the things that really matter. Set your priorities. The rest is just sand."

The Code

From the Roman legionnaire to the Japanese Samurai, from the French *chevalier* to the Spanish *caballero*, the figure mounted on a horse embodies honor and pride. Twelfth century writers noted this in their tales of knights in shining armor. Whatever the time, whatever the tribe or national identity, the figure on horseback has had a special status among people. And the true figure on horseback resists betraying that status. The myth becomes reality when one understands that. Nowhere is that status, the code of the horseman, more evident than the figure of the cowboy.

It has been posited that the large belt buckles, chaps, vests and high boots are all vestiges of the armor worn by knights. Whether or not that is true, one thing is clear. The cowboy lives by a code as old as the earliest figures on horseback. The one thing in common they have is the shame one must endure when they are dismounted. Old cowboys I have known resist doing anything that cannot be done on horseback. In fact, many reject using tractors and trucks to handle work they could do from the back of a horse. It is part of their unwritten ingrained code.

Among the things they do not want to do is ride the honey truck, let alone filling it with a pitchfork. Many do not even want to ride in a hearse when they die. Like the old folk song says, "When I die take my saddle down from the wall. Put it on my pony and lead him from the stall. Tie my bones to his back and face us to the west. And we'll ride the prairie that we love the best."

Some claim this code dates back to the tales of King Arthur and the story of Lancelot who dismounts from his horse and rides in a peasant's cart to gain access to a castle to save a damsel in distress. It does not matter how many villains he kills in the process or how many ladies he saves. In the end, he is identified by the shameful term, "The knight who once rode in a peasant's cart."

So it is with the cowboy. Take him off the horse and he walks his bandy leg stride with a kind of confused amble. Bowed legs are pretensions. He never planned it that they be that way. They are simply the result of all the years in the saddle. The bruises and broken bones from accidents on horseback are more than reminders of those events, the serve as a kind of badge that identifies their place in the world. No wonder kids dream of being up there on the back of a fine horse surveying the rest of the world. May their numbers increase.

Wrangler

When I was teenage ranch hand in Colorado, I was approached by a hunting out-fitter who offered me a contract to drive a herd of horses twenty-six miles to a jumping off place where the hunters would meet the outfitter and head for the hills.

That's right, drive a herd of horses. The only trailers around then were those pulled by semi-trailer trucks. Folks just rode or drove their stock from place to place when possible.

I took the contract to the move the herd of saddle and packhorses to Twin Lakes from a ranch near Buena Vista. To get the job done I hired a couple boys at lose ends, there were a lot of us at loose ends in those days. They were outriders and rode drag while I rode point. It was a trip we had to make in one day, so we had no time to lose.

We took our rigging and caught three of the horses, saddled them and mounted up. After some initial rough riding on horses that had been on the range for some time, we lined out the herd of two dozen horses and headed north at a leisurely pace. It was a different time. The ranches along the way had cattle guards and gates we could use as we moved through the upper Arkansas Valley without ever having to take to the road.

There were water tanks along the way that the Colorado autumn had not fro-zen over. At lunchtime, we stopped to take our lunches out of saddlebags and eat, while the horses helped themselves to some grass. We ate, stuffed our litter in sad-dlebags, and headed them north. It was about dusk when we arrived at the wait-ing corral at Twin Lakes. The outfitter was there to pay us and haul us back home. We got off and walked stiff-legged like real cowboys, loaded our rigging in his truck and climbed into the cab four abreast.

Although it was an uneventful day, it was one a youngster hangs onto as the years pass. I am not sure why, but in the west a day's work well done is mark of manhood. Maybe that is why we remember.

Odds and Ends

A Quilt of Life

I know many quilters. The Aiken Homemakers that met at Principio Church and my sister, Barbara Ellen, in Kansas are quilters. Miss Susan and my grandmothers were quilters. They love their work. They know all the designs and what they mean. I have slept under many homemade quilts. I heard this story about a quilt that sort of stuck with me. Hope you enjoy it.

"As I faced my Maker at the last Judgment, I was the last one to kneel before God. Every one of us had laid out our lives like the squares of a quilt. Angels sat before each of us sewing our squares together into a quilt that would reflect our life.

But, as my Angel took each piece of cloth off the pile, I noticed how ragged and empty each of my squares was. They were filled with giant holes. Each square was labeled with a part of my life that had been difficult, the challenges and temptations I was faced with in everyday life. I saw hardships that I had endured, which were the largest holes of all.

I glanced around me. Nobody else had such squares. Other than a tiny hole here and there, the other quilts were filled with rich color and the bright hues of worldly fortune. I gazed upon my own life and was disheartened. My Angel was sewing the ragged pieces of cloth together, threadbare and empty, like binding air.

Finally the time came when each quilt of life was to be displayed, held up to the light, the scrutiny of truth. The others rose, each in turn, holding up their quilts. Their lives had been filled with wonderful things. And then it was time for me to show my quilt. I was ashamed. I hadn't had all the earthly fortunes. I had love in my life, and laughter. But there had also been trials of illness and death and struggles that mad me have to start over many times. I struggled with the temptation to quit, only to somehow muster the strength to pick up and begin again. I had prayed many times for help and guidance in my life. I had endured ridicule.

Each time I offered it up to God in hopes that I would not melt within my skin beneath the judgmental gaze of those who unfairly judged me. And now, I had to face the truth. My life was what it was, and I had to accept it for what it had been.

I got up all stiff and slow and lifted the ragged squares of my life to the light. An awe-filled gasp filled the air. I gazed around at the others who stared at me with eyes wide. Then, I looked at the quilt me. Light flooded the many holes, creating an image. It was the face of Christ. Then our Lord stood before me, with warmth and love in His eyes.

He said, "Every time you gave over your life to me, it became my life, My hardships, and My struggles. Each point of light in your life is when you stepped aside and let Me shine through, until there was more of Me than there was of you."

What a nice story. May all your quilts be threadbare and worn, allowing Christ to shine through as you ride on.

A Sense of Community

Like a lot folks in these troubled times I have been pondering the loss of community. In the rat race we have allowed to emerge and exist, a sense of community is clearly missing. Those of us raised in a time when neighbors helped one another farming, helped one another without being asked, helped one another in town and country, miss those days. And with good reason.

To that end, I have been reading some work by Wendell Berry. With over forty books under his belt as an author, poet, essayist and Kentucky farmer Wendell Berry says real community is a place that includes all of its native and naturalized inhabitants. He says, "The human part of it would be responsibly conscious of the having-in-common of which the community is composed."

Community and place are the same, Berry reminds us. That is, geography is important. What professionals call "networking communities" are simply metaphors for community. They aren't really communities. The reason: We need to be rooted in a place even if we are relatively new comers. Berry says we have to give up on trying to escape our troubles and our messes we ourselves have created. In fact, he says, the idea of preserving rural America is not succeeding. Why? He illuminates the question by describing how "it is almost impossible, economically, to preserve good farmland, good farming, or even good farmers." He says this as he reminds us that we haven't even asked the hard question: how long will we survive without them?

Confronting all the efforts at historic preservation and the movement to save farmland, he says they are all good, but the are not enough. No movement, no organization, no organized efforts are achieving their goal according to Berry. The reason is simple, he says. "The present economy is inherently destructive of land and other necessities." "The way to save farmland," he says, "is by farming it well." Therefore, "it is necessary to save farmers who know how to farm well."

One of his examples of farming well is the Amish. He notes, "There are prosperous Amish farms of 100 acres or less. A few acres of vegetables can provide a decent income, given a decent market."

That was brought to my attention more than thirty years ago when an organic farmer in my parish in Kansas was raising more crops per acre on a small eighty-acre farm than his neighbor who farmed a large farm using chemical fertilizers, huge tractors and machinery and all the stuff of which big farms are made. It is a cultural thing requiring major philosophical changes in a farmer's thinking.

The bottom line seems to be this—urban communities eat and rural communities raise the food they eat They should not be in competition with each other. Capitalistic thinking that cheap good, regardless of its quality, is wrong. Giving Berry the last word, "We have to think of local food economies based on cooperation between consumers and producers."

Ain't It Funny

Blind Tom, the preacher man, came by the other day. After saying 'howdy' to Rags and Beans he sat down at the kitchen table and sipped on an iced tea while he muttered,

"Ain't it funny how we set our clocks to arise at 4:00 am or 5:00 am to be at the job by 7:30; yet, when Sunday comes we can't get to church for the 11:00 a.m. service to praise the one who gave us the jobs!"

I had to admit he had a point, but he wasn't finished. He leaned back and said, "I've been doing a lot of thinking about a lot of things and it seems to me that it is funny how we call God our Father and Jesus our brother; but find it hard to introduce them to our family."

I chuckled and said, "I'm always struck by how small our personal sins seem, but how the sins of others are huge."

Rags said, "I find it pretty funny how we demand justice for others; but expect mercy in our case."

Beans jumped right in with, "Ain't it funny how much difficulty some have learning the gospel well enough to tell others; but how simple it is to understand and explain the latest gossip about someone else."

"That's strikes close to home," Rags said. "And I think its funny how we can't think of anything to say when we pray; but don't have any difficulty thinking of things to talk about to a friend."

Blind Tom said, "It's also pretty funny how we are so quick to take directions from a total stranger when we are lost; but are hesitant to take God's direction for our lives."

Rags said, "I get a kick out of how so many church goers sing "Standing on the Promises"; when all they do is sit on the premises."

Beans came back with, "I am annoyed by how people want God to answer their prayers; but refuse to listen to God's counsel when it conflicts with their own ideas."

"Yeah, "Rags said, "and some folks sing about heaven; but live only for today. And they talk about how they are going to Heaven; and think there is no Hell."

Blind Tom got a second wind and said, "Its also funny how it is okay to blame God for evil and suffering in the world; but it is not necessary to thank Him for what is good and pleasant."

Rags was caught up in the spirit of the moment and he came up with, "Ain't it funny how when something goes wrong we cry, "Lord, why me?"; but when something goes right, we think, "Hey! I really came through!"

Blind Tom had enough, finished his tea, and got up to leave. His final words were, "I make a little comment and you old boys just go crazy. I believe I'll keep my opinions to myself after this."

As he went out the kitchen door Rags yelled after him, "Ride on, preacher, ride on."

An American Vision

I have been thinking a lot about how all of us, unless we are descendants of native Americans, are the children of immigrants. I have been thinking about that and how good fortune smiled on my English ancestors in the late seventeenth century when they immigrated to what is now North Carolina and one married into the Cherokee Nation. It also smiled on my Irish ancestors in the nineteenth century and on my numerous German ancestors who started coming in the mid-eighteenth century and kept coming into the mid-nineteenth century. Good fortune, indeed.

The Irish had to put up with several generations of prejudice and nativistic ignorance. My German ancestors struggled to assimilate early in this century so they might escape the hangman's rope during World War I. Yes, Virginia, they hung German-Americans in the Midwest in fits of that same nativistic ignorance and fear. But, I still see possibilities in these United States for justice that rolls down like the waters and righteousness like an ever flowing stream.

I have always had a special place in my heart for an immigrant son named Carl Sandburg. I like what he wrote back in 1953. "I see America, not in the setting sun of a black night of despair ahead of us. I see America in the crimson light of a rising sun fresh from the burning, creative hand of God. I see great days ahead, great days possible to men and women of vision."

The key word is vision. That has always been true for people of faith. Even Henry Kissinger, for whom I have little regard, put his finger on it when he said, "For other nations, Utopia is a blessed past never to be recovered; for Americans, it is just beyond the horizon."

I am not sure about Utopia. That may be a little grandiose. But I think possibilities little dreamed of await us if we have vision. You see, people of faith, do not allow the poor to be beaten down, children to be punished for the weaknesses of their parents, minorities to be targets of mean-spirited politics. The British statesman Lord Grey once wrote, "The United States is like a gigantic broiler. Once the fire is lighted under it, there is no limit to the power it can generate."

People of faith who live in this nation, people of vision who see the possibilities, will not allow the pain to continue. Theodore Roosevelt put his finger on it.

He said, "This country will not be a good place for any of us to live in unless we make it a good place for all of us to live in."

And in his inordinate wisdom, Adlai Stevenson said, "America is much more than a geographical fact. It is a political and moral fact—the first community in which man set out in principle to institutionalize freedom, responsible government and human equality."

The significant word in that is moral. So, check your cinch and ride on.

And Now a Word about Mules

Back in 1952 while the Korean War was going on, I decided to join the army and become a hero like Audie Murphy. Like him and many other enlistees throughout our history, I was a poor, rural boy with not much future. Therefore, I went to see an army recruiter. Like all recruiters, he stretched the truth, which is a kind way of saying "he lied." The dialogue went something like this.

"What would you like to do in the army?"

"I have worked with horses all my life. I would like to be a cavalryman."

"There is no horse cavalry anymore, son."

"I would sure like to work with horses."

"Tell you what; the army has a mountain pack mule artillery unit at Camp Carson, Colorado. How would that do?"

"That would be great."

"Sign here."

I did. After basic training at Ft. Riley, Kansas, with the Tenth Mountain Division, they handed me orders to report to Camp Carson. Oh, boy, I thought the adventure is about to begin.

At Camp Carson, I discovered I was indeed assigned to an artillery unit. However, it was a .155 Long Tom unit, not a mountain artillery pack mule unit. That unit no longer exists; they told me when I complained. Now, folks who know me know I don't take kindly to being messed around with, so I began to complain every day to my sergeant. And then one day, the 19th Military Police Command, a CID and prison unit, sent out word that they needed bodies to fill some of their empty spaces. My sergeant enthusiastically recommended me. I wound up in the military police.

A few days ago, I was researching the history of Camp Carson (now Ft. Carson) and discovered the mountain mule artillery unit wasn't disbanded until 1956—four and one-half years after I enlisted. They lied to me twice.

The mule units had been there since World War II. The first shipment of mules arrived from Nebraska on July 30, 1942. The soldiers trained them to carry a field pack over almost inaccessible terrain. It took six to eight weeks to train a mule and the battle between man and beast could be, folks said, "spectacular."

Two mules stood out in those units. One was a goldbricker named Useless. They tried to turn him into a good "soldier," but it was useless. He was first a pack mule. Then a messenger mule. Then they hitched him to a wagon and used to haul hay, but even hay hauling was too much for Useless.

However, one mule stood out from the rest. He was a white mule named Hamilton T. Bone ("Hambone"). He was the pride of the 4th Field Artillery Battalion. Year after year, he carried the First Sergeants of the 4th up Ute Pass to Camp Hale at 10,000 feet near Leadville. Sometimes they went along the foothills of the Rockies to Cheyenne, Wyoming for the Frontier Days Rodeo. His silvery-white coat and entertaining antics as a jumper won him fame in July 1949 when Life *Magazine* printed a feature story on the four-footed soldier.

After serving 13 years at Carson, Hambone was retired involuntarily along with 331 other mules in December, 1956, replaced by helicopters. Hambone spent his retirement years as a star attraction with the Pikes Peak or Bust Rodeo and the Pikes Peak Range Ride. When Hambone showed signs of advanced age, he was returned to Fort Carson where he died a few months later. Miss Susan and I lived in Colorado Springs at the time and his death made newspaper headlines. He was buried with military honors in front of Division Artillery Headquarters. A memorial of stone quarried on the reservation, was erected over his grave. Another hero dead and gone.

As Everyone Knows

"As everyone knows, the first Christians drank eggnog when Christ was born, and ate marshmallow birds when He died: So it was written, so it shall be done," said Blind Tom, the Preacher. when he stopped by Wishitwerea Ranch.

He is retired, but I often ask him questions about traditions among Christians that have developed over the centuries. We do this when he stops by, because 1) he is a good old boy and an iconoclast and 2) Because there is so much junk in modern Christian dogma I am on the verge of losing all interest.

"Maybe you can explain Easter eggs," I said.

"Nope," he replied. "All I know is they started in Europe when folks gave gifts to children at Easter time. They didn't have any money, so I heard, but they had hens and eggs, so they boiled eggs, colored them and gave them to the children."

"Why didn't they boil the hens and color them and give them to children?" I asked.

"Don't mention it," he said. "Some idiot will do it just to make a few bucks. They already put dye on baby chicks and ducks and sell them to unsuspecting parents to give their children, so the child can watch the little chick or duckling die from being dyed and handled like a stuffed toy."

"Yup, I've seen that," I said. "They do the same thing with rabbits."

"Dye them?"

"Nope, sell them to unsuspecting parents so their kids can handle them to death."

"Doesn't have much to do with one's religious faith does it?' he asked.

"Not much, but it sure helps out retailers."

"How about all them other "religious" days like Father's Day, Grandparent's Day, Mother's Day?" He asked rhetorically.

"Hallmark," I said.

"Right," he responded. "Good for card and flower sales."

"So, how do we recognize a real holy day and how should we celebrate it?"

"Each morning when we wakeup and face the rising sun is a holy day," he said. "We celebrate by loving creation as we love ourselves."

"Sounds kind of like what traditional Indians believe," I said.

"It does," he said. "Never understood why the missionaries tried so hard to separate them from their faith when they had it right all along."

"You better be careful," I suggested. "They might toss you out of the church."

"Right," he said. "Maybe, they'll force me into retirement."

He got up and left with a smile on face. I watched him bandy-leg his way out to his old pick-em-truck and get in to drive away. He rolled down the window and with a wave shouted, "Check your cinch and ride on."

Backporch Musings on Prejudice

Rags Bandy and Old Beans Taylor came one day after church.

"Blind Tom said today we need to be clear eyed about the recent terrorist attacks and think in rational ways," Old Beans said. "He said we shouldn't allow prejudice towards Arabs or Muslims to cloud our minds and cause us to do stupid things."

Blind Tom Harper is the preacher at Whatzup Methodist Church.

Rags chewed on a toothpick and said, "We need to smack somebody for this horrible deal."

"Seems like," Old Beans said, "but Blind Tom is pretty smart for a Methodist.

"I guess so," Rags answered.

They sat down in my back porch rocking chairs and sort of stared off into space.

"You know," I said, "I have a tough time with any kind of prejudice because its usually based on fear and ignorance. But, I also understand that most folks like to have someone else to blame for their misfortunes. You old boys know that we Americans have hated everyone at some time throughout our history."

"I guess it started with the Indians," Rags mused. "After they taught us how to farm and survive in this country."

"Yeah," Old Beans said. "I n my own time we have been what they call schizophrenic about enemies. We have hated the Germans, Irish, Blacks, Japanese, Italians, Catholics, and now Muslims."

"Why?" I asked.

"Doggone if I know. Just kind of dumb, ain't it?"

Rags was still chewing on his toothpick.

"Now some good old boy jerks are attacking folks in their own neighborhoods. Folks who had nothing to do with these attacks," he offered. "Blind Tom says we are all Americans and we need to be working together instead of blaming each other."

"Blind Tom said that was just ignorance loose in the world and that such ignorance is what gives birth to other kinds of evil," Old Beans looked out across the yard at our pine trees and reached for his Barlow knife. "Said we ought to go on with our lives. Said we need to be clear eyed and rational. Got anything to whittle on, Vern."

I reached into a box of firewood and handed him a piece of pine. He sat there shaving thin strips of the wood. Rags pointed out to the barn.

"Gonna paint that sucker some day?"

"I guess," I said.

"Blind Tom is a good preacher. He sees pretty good for a blind man," Old Beans said.

"He shore does," Rags added. "Know any Arabs, Vern"

"Yep," I answered. "Even rode a camel once on a hill up above the Garden of Gethsemane."

Rags grinned and said, "Ride on, Hoss, ride on."

Bad Day at Wishitwerea Ranch

Elmo Musgrave came by one day and he was as nervous as a cowboy at a black tie reception. He sat down in the kitchen and took the cup of coffee I offered him. He sat there silently sipping and starring out the window with a vacant look in his eyes.

"You look pitiful," I said.

He just nodded.

"So, tell me what's up."

He took a deep breath and another sip of coffee.

"Frogs," he said.

"Frogs?"

"Yep. Frogs."

"What about frogs?"

"Their sex organs are in danger."

Now I have heard many strange things from my *compadres*. This is a new one. I pressed on.

"You are going to have to clarify that a little for me," I said.

"Well," he took a deep breath, "we are spraying this weed killer al over the country. We spray it on lawns, fields, gardens, along the road, on golf courses. And its making frogs hermaphrodites."

"What do we call this chemical?" I asked.

"Atrazine."

"Never heard of it."

"Well, its out there in all kinds of fancy weed killers. When it rains, it runs off into our ditches, creek, rivers, and ponds. In fact, it even gets into our drinking water."

"Our drinking water?" He had my attention.

"Right. In the ground water as well as streams. We are drinking this stuff, Hoss."

"Where did you hear about this?"

"National Academy of Science reported it. I read it in the newspaper. Back pages, buried. You know how they are."

I nodded and poured him a little more coffee.

"How does this mess up the sexual organs of frogs?"

"The report said it causes male frog cells to produce an enzyme that converts testosterone in estrogen. This destroys their reproductivity."

"That makes sense," I said. "What do the scientists say about how it may endanger human beings?"

"You mean folks like us?"

"Right. Human beings."

"Well, the research chief said, 'I'm not saying it's safe for humans. I'm not saying it's unsafe for humans. All I'm saying is that it makes hermaphrodites of frogs.'"

"That sounds ominous, I guess."

"Yep," he said as he got up and walked gingerly to the door where he turned and said, "It sure does make me nervous."

I nodded affirmatively and watched him walk to his pick-em-up truck and drive away. Atrazine. Frogs. I think I'll just go back to bed.

Beards

Someone asked me why I wear a beard. I have many reasons. I make them up as I go along. The literary one is that I use Walt Whitman as my model. His face, not his poetry, claims my attention. The wise eyes, the beard, the wide brimmed hat provide a definite presence as he peers out of his photos into the eyes of the beholder. Besides, I want to stroll eccentric in streets of the commonplace where people stare at old men with walking sticks, that third leg to balance the form, children smile and wave, believing he may be Santa Claus bearing gifts hidden in a coat tattered by long years on the road. That is the literary reason. The real reason may be something else.

Miss Susan says she prefers me with a beard. One of my daughters suggests that may be because anything covering face is an improvement. One purported friend says that if that is true then I should wear a paper bag over my head. However, the truth can be found elsewhere. I have always disliked shaving. When my beard starting turning silver like my hair I jumped at the chance to be different. Now, it seems everyone wears a beard.

I have to say I was trying out the style of beards many young folks, athletes, and others are wearing back in sixties. You know the one, mustache and chin whiskers. It is called a beaver beard after Lord Beaverbrook who wore one with distinction.

Full beards, of course have been around for hundreds of years. Pioneers, mountain men, farmers, and the like wore them for a couple of reasons: warmth and the lack of opportunity or tools with which to shave.

So, I wear a beard and that is just the way it goes.

Buffalo

My physician told me I needed to watch my cholesterol. So, I've been trying and then I did some research and discovered a sure way to decrease fat and negative cholesterol, while providing high iron and protein content in the diet. It is simple. Eat like an Indian. The staple diet for hundreds of years for tens of thousands of Native Americans was buffalo.

The American Bison (buffalo) numbered in the tens of millions until indiscriminate slaughter by white men and the U.S. Army rendered the American buffalo nearly extinct by 1900. In fact, there were only 13 live American Bison left and they were all in the Yellowstone Park area.

Because popular culture identifies the bison with the west, many folks do not know bison existed in the eastern part of the country at the time of the original colonial settlers. They ranged much of the continent including as far north as Canada's Northwest Territories and Mexico in the south. The press of European arrivals soon resulted in their extermination in the peripheries of their territory east of the Mississippi. They were extinct in the east by 1833.

When my ancestors homesteaded on the high plains of Kansas between the Solomon and Republican rivers shortly after the War Between the States, their farm lay along the eastern edge of the bison grazing grounds. While my grandfather, a Civil War veteran was breaking sod in hopes of creating a new future, frustrated Cheyenne, Arapaho, Comanche and Kiowa were meeting with United States representatives at the southern edge of Kansas along a creek named Medicine Lodge. The purpose: narrow the region where the Indian might live and hunt bison as they had for generations. The treaty, like all others was made to be broken.

By then, bison herds were decreasing. Professional hunters working for the railroads killed them to feed railroad construction crews. So-called sportsmen took trains from Kansas City and other points east and gleefully shot the animals from railroad car windows never bothering to disembark to butcher the animals. They shot them just to see them crumple and fall. Hunters for commercial butchering businesses also did their part to decimate the herds.

Indians were not without blame. For most of their history, bison were killed by the tribes for their needs, but their concept of an endless supply of necessities on the hoof led them to sometimes take only the tongue if they were in a hurry. There were times when they also maneuvered great herds over cliffs where the animals fell to their deaths to be selectively butchered. One estimate is that Native Americans were eating only four out of every 100 bison they killed. Then, as trade with Europeans became more important, they began killing bison taking only their hides and tongues to exchange for trade goods. By the 1840s, the number of hides prepared for trade was far greater than those used by the Indians themselves. In 1839, the American Fur Company bought 45,000 buffalo robes and 67,000 the next year, representing a staggering amount of labor by Indian hide workers.

Another aspect important to consider when one studies the decline of the bison herds is that hunters who took the animals for food killed cows almost exclusively. The reason was simple. Their meat was superior to the bulls. Consequently, many herds had three to four times as many bulls as cows. So it is that the great herds of bison were doomed. It was only a matter of time before entrepreneurs began developing other uses for bison products when accelerated their decline.

The primary uses for hides were for lap robes, overcoats, cold-weather gauntlets, belts for driving machines and such. And that market was in the east. The slow tanning process was not economically profitable for commercial markets until 1871, when a new method of tanning developed by a New England tanner produced excellent leather. That development accelerated the destruction of the American bison as the market value of bison hides shot up. The first three thousand shipped east in 1872 brought $3.50 each, a total of $10,500. The value of bison hides created a rush bringing all sorts of hunters to the plains. Dodge City, at the end of the Atchison, Topeka and Santa Fe Railroad, became the capitol of the hide hunting rage.

By 1893, an estimated 300 American Bison (*Bison bison*) were all that was left of the herds that numbered from 30 to 1000 million in A.D. 1500. Whatever their numbers, thousands, if not tens of thousands, froze to death in blizzards, drowned crossing rivers and creeks of ice, or they simply mired down in muddy bogs.

Moving seasonally south and back north through the plains, it seemed that there would be no end to what this mobile commissary provided. Some have called them the Indian Wal-Mart, provided the Indians with food, clothing, lodging, eating and sewing utensils and myriads of other necessities. A bison bull might weigh more than 2,000 pounds and provide about 800 pounds of useable meat. Cows weighed from 700 to 1,200 pounds, and provided an average of 400 pounds of meat. Horns were fashioned into spoons or scoops, arrow points, powder horns, medication and decorative headdresses. Fat was used as a lubricant and soap. Bones became knives, pipes, arrowheads, splints, shovels and war clubs. Tails were used for ornaments, but also as a fly brush or whip. Muscles and sinew became glue, thread and arrow ties. Hoofs became glue. Hair was used in headdresses and for ropes, padding and moccasin lining. Gall and blood was used for paint. The extra thick hide on the top of the head became a bowl. The beard and teeth were used for ornaments. The bladder became a medicine bag. The scrotum was useful as a rattle container. The heart was used as a sack to carry dried meat. Later, these hides became a thriving trade item. The stomach served as a water bag or cooking pot. The tanned hides became moccasins, buckets, drumheads, ropes, saddles and stirrups, snowshoes and tipi coverings.

Methods of hide hunters ranged from a single individual to large organized hunting camps that developed systems by which to increase the kill and the harvest of hides. Many men, some later famous, earned their keep as "stinking" hide hunters including the Earps, Mastersons and one who would come to be called Buffalo Bill Cody.

These hide hunters were small fry compared with some. In 35 days in 1873, Tom Nixon killed 2,173. A hunter name Zack Light killed 2,300 in a one year period. The soon to be famous law officer Bill Tilghman shot and killed over 3,300 from September 1873 to April 1874. Brick Bond averaged 300 kills daily over a 60-day period with a total of 5,853. For three years, a hunter named Jim Cator killed 4,000 annually. J. Wright Moar, brother to an eastern tanner killed 20,500 over a six-year period beginning in 1871.

A year of national financial panic in 1873 brought the value of the hides down to 80 cents to $1.50. A year later the price dropped to one dollar for bull hides, sixty cents for cowhides and forty cents for calf hides. Still the hunter kept hunting and struggling farmers and others of every occupation saw a chance to make ends meet by engaging in the massive slaughter of bison.

There was no escape for the bison. Knowing the law protected bison from white hunters in areas reserved for the Indians, a group of hunters approached Colonel Richard Irving Dodge at Ft. Dodge to ask him what the punishment might be if they left Kansas and went south into the Texas panhandle. The Colonel hesitated, probably thinking over the policies established by his superiors, Generals Philip Sheridan and William Tecumseh Sherman, and then commented, "If I were a buffalo hunter, I would hunt where the buffalo are." So it was, that the devastation of the herds on the Kansas plains moved south to continue the slaughter with the army looking the other way.

An estimated 850,000 bison hides were shipped from Dodge City in the years 1872–1874. After another four years of slaughter, the great herds were decimated. The hunters looked up one day to discover that their quarry had all but disappeared. The only thing left to mark the passing of millions bison was bones. The nightmare of rotting, putrid carcasses strung out across the plains became a vista of bones.

Dodge City, the "Buffalo Capital" for three years, became the gathering place for heaps of bleached bones gathered from across a prairie once littered with decaying carcasses. Homesteaders, during hard times, gathered the bones and sold them for six to eight dollars a ton to eastern buyers. Huge bone piles collected along the railroad towering into the sky as carload after carload hauled the bones east to be used in the manufacture of china, bone char and phosphorus fertilizer. The apparent end of the American Bison loomed on the horizon.

Demise of the American Bison was partly grounded in a systemic disregard of the interrelationships of organisms and their environment. Some Indians believed that when bison disappeared for a season they went to lake-bottom grasslands and when they reappeared, they came from those habitats. Some saw bison emerge from caves, or knew of others who witnessed this, and believed that was where they went before coming back again to the plains. Such beliefs had fundamental conceptual ecological and environmental consequences. One is reminded of fishermen, oystermen, and others who disregard ecological impacts believing that their quarry will always return.

Plains Indian ecological understanding was never within the parameters of western ideas of an ecosystem. Therefore, it is easy to see how a belief of this nature would get in the way of conservation of a declining resource on the nineteenth-century plains. If bison did not return when they were expected or in the numbers anticipated, it was not because too many were being killed but because they had not left their lake-bottom prairies or their caves. How could one kill too many if one held to this belief? How could they possibly become extinct?

The size of the herds was also affected by predation, disease, fires which maimed and killed animals, climate, competition from horses for the valuable grass, the market, and other factors. Most significant was drought. It was severe prior to the fifteenth century and episodic in the eighteenth. In the nineteenth century, it reoccurred often and may have been worst at the very moment when other pressures converged in the early years of the decades from 1840 to 1880, thereby hastening the destruction of the herds. Yet no matter the impact from drought, horses, or fires, what seemed to doom the bison most were the commodities markets for buffalo tongues, skins, meat, and robes and the railroads.

The time of the American Bison seemed to be over by the turn of twentieth century. On occasion, however, some were spotted in remote areas of the Great Plains. But, all was not lost. Concerned individuals turned their attention to the recovery of the bison and nearly a century later their numbers would begin increasing. Ranches throughout the west have dispensed with cattle and now raise large herds of buffalo. However, the true day of the American Bison was over.

It seemed that never again would the magnificence of their swaying tide of life surge across the prairies. And yet, today there are over 250,000 buffalo with about 230,000 of them being raised on private ranches. They are range animals eating grass and living outside feedlots. I reiterate—no growth-inducing hormones or steroids.

Buffalo has a rich, beef-like taste. I know I've eaten it. Sometimes it tastes a little sweet, but that's okay with me. It is lower in cholesterol and calories yet higher in iron, protein, and other essential vitamins. Therefore, it is a perfect beef substitute for the health-conscious. In fact, buffalo has less cholesterol than chicken with the skin removed or even fish! Look at this data.

Studies done at many major universities, (Cornell University, the University of Utah, the University of South Dakota, Pennsylvania State University, and the University of Bristol in England) confirm that buffalo is very high in essential fatty acids. It has an excellent ratio of Omega-3 to Omega-6 acids and contains much more conjugated linoleic acid than was previously known. There is 90% less fat, 50% less cholesterol, 30% higher in protein and has less calories. There are no known human allergies. It is higher in iron than any other meat. There are no problems with E-Coli in buffalo.

Folks with heart disease can be helped by buffalo meat! LDL cholesterol levels may be reduced by 40–45% over about a 6-month period by eating only 5 ounces of Buffalo meat 4–5 times per week. Take that McDonalds!

Nutritional values of buffalo reads thusly: a 3 oz. serving has 93 calories, 1.8 grams of fat, and 43 mg. cholesterol. Turkey has 125 calories, 3 grams of fat, and 55 mg. of cholesterol. Beef has 183 calories, 8.7 grams of fat, and 55 mg. of cholesterol. Chicken has 140 calories, 3 grams of fat, and 73 mg. of cholesterol. Fish has 125 calories, 3 grams of fat, and 59 mg. of cholesterol.

You cook it much like beef. Often, the taste in indistinguishable from beef. It is not gamey or wild tasting. Buffalo tends to be darker and richer in color than many of the other red meats. Lack of fat means buffalo meat cooks faster.

So, I am going to move in that direction. Hey, Doc, its time to put buffalo on your list of diets.

Burning Questions

Being a curious sort I have always asked a lot of questions in my life. Sometimes they have been annoying to others. At other times they have just been considered weird. I thought I would share with you some thought provoking questions that I have either asked or heard.

1. If a book about failure doesn't sell, is it a best seller?

2. Do cemetery workers prefer the graveyard shift?

3. What do you so when you see an endangered animal eating endangered plants?

4. Is it possible to be totally impartial?

5. What's another word for thesaurus?

6. If a parsley farmer is sued, can they garnish his wages?

7. Would a fly without wings be called a walk?

8. Why do steam irons have permanent press settings?

9. Can you be a closet claustrophobic?

10. Why do they lock gas station toilets? Are they afraid someone will clean them?

11. Why do people who know the least know it the loudest?

12. If a funeral procession is at night, do the people drive with their lights off?

13. If a stealth bomber crashes in the forest, will it make a sound?

14. When it rains, why don't sheep shrink?

15. Should vegetarians eat animal crackers?

16. If the police arrest a mime, do they tell him he has the right to remain silent?

17. Why is the word abbreviation so long?

18. When companies ship Styrofoam, what do they pack it in?

19. How come so many right to life people are for war and capital punishment?

Church Squirrels

In my old friend Tater Johnson's hometown, there are three country churches: Presbyterian, United Methodist, and Roman Catholic. A few years ago, it seems that each church had a bell tower and ceiling overrun with annoying squirrels. Like always three different approaches were taken to solve the problems.

The Presbyterians called a meeting of the Session to decide what to do about the squirrels. After much prayer and consideration, these dedicated church folks determined that the squirrels were predestined to be there and they should not interfere with God's divine will.

The United Methodists, like always, formed a committee to decide the action to take. After weeks of meetings, they decided that they were not in a position to harm any of God's creations. Therefore, they humanely trapped the squirrels and set them free a few miles outside of town. Three days later, the squirrels were back.

The Catholics, however, were able to come up with the best and most effective solution. One morning they caught the squirrels. The priest baptized each squirrel in great danger to himself and then the squirrels were named and registered as members of the church. That did it. Now they only see the squirrels on Christmas and Easter.

Death and Dying

At the risk of seeming ghoulish, I thought I would share a little history with you. At a recent conference, the historical language of the west was discussed. One area covered was that of death and dying. The roots of some curious slang emerged. In 1698, an undertaker was being called a dismal trader. By 1859, the term land broker emerged and by 1875, the term cold cook signified an undertaker. Carrion hunter was the label by 1880.

The 1650 term "hearse" became "cold meat cart" in 1820 in the west and the "dead wagon" by 1894.

Funeral was a term established in 1523. By 1634, the term weeper (a professional mourner) becomes common. In 1780, reference to a funeral gave us the words "last compliment." The term cold cook shop (funeral parlor) came about by five years later. Funerary (photos of the deceased) came into common use by 1855 and that evolved into "funeralize" (to preach) by 1859. The terms "lay 'em down," "black job" and "send-off" became synonymous with the funeral in 1880. Then in 1908, some wag established then term "cold meat party."

The term cemetery came into being in 1400. Potter's field is the term established in 1777 as a graveyard for the poor or unknown. In 1808, a cemetery was called the "burying hill." By 1820, the word for grave became bury hole. A Spanish term emerged in 1856—campo santo. Bone orchard emerged in 1872. The year 1880 was a rich one for cemetery names. They include grave patch, still lot, land-yard, and last home. The terms comfort station and still hill were added in 1900.

Coffin words are as unusual as all the others. In 1799 it was called a "bone house." The next year folks called it slumbercot. Throughout the nineteenth century words for coffin included cold meat box, casket, burial case, wooden overcoat, pine overcoat, eternity box, painted box, and box.

Death itself has many names. In the nineteenth century, they included the great equalizer, the great adventure, bedtime, the last roundup, the long trail, no breakfast, the big jump, the everlasting knock, the grand secret, Old Mr. Grim, 30 (from the telegrapher's code for the end—journalists still use it), the smokey shore, and the misty beyond. Beginning in 1900 the grand bounce and the payoff joined the linguistic terms for death.

I was fascinated by the historical terms used to signify someone was on the brink of death. The language guy said they mean "Not dead yet—but give it a minute." These terms included booked, death damps, goner, flush out, croaker, dropping like flies, last gasp, the rattles, and death bell.

Some of the western terms brought a smile to my lips. If you died of rope croup it meant you died of the disease of hanging. Human fruit or cottonwood blossom was what they called you if you were found hanging in a tree. To dance on air and dance on nothing refers to the act of getting hung. Vigilantes were called hemp committees who had necktie parties or frolics, hanging bees and Texas cakewalks.

Enough of this—so ride on.

Deer Hunting in the Wild West

It was Saturday morning when Jake, an avid hunter, woke up eager to go bag the first deer of the season. He went to the kitchen to get a cup of coffee and to his surprise found his wife, Alice, sitting there, fully dressed in camouflage.

"What are you up to?" Jake asked

Alice smiled and responded, "We've been talking about spending more time together, so I'm going deer hunting with you!"

Jake had many reservations about this; however, he reluctantly decided to take her along. Three hours later they arrive at a game preserve outside of San Marcos, Texas. Jake sat his lovely wife safely up in the tree stand and said, "If you see a deer, take careful aim on it and I'll come running back as soon as I hear the shot."

He walked away with a smile on his face knowing that Alice was such a bad shot she could not hit an elephant—much less a deer. Not ten minutes passed before he is startled as he heard an array of gunshots. He quickly ran back. As he got close to her stand, he heard Alice screaming, "Get away from my deer!"

Confused and frightened Jake ran faster towards his screaming tree bound wife. Again he heard her yell, "Get away from my deer now!" followed by another volley of gunfire!

By now, Jake was within sight of where he had left his wife up a tree and he was surprised to see a tall Texas cowboy standing with his hands high in the air. He was dusty and frazzled from a hard ride after some brush bound cattle. And Jake saw something in his eyes he had never seen in a cowboy's eyes—pure unadulterated fear. As Jake drew close to the tree stand, he overheard the obviously distraught, the cowboy saying, "Okay, lady! You can stop shooting. And you can have your deer! Just let me get my saddle off it!"

Do Not Call the Dead

Rags came one day while I was feeding the horses. He was waving a newspaper in my face and he looked apoplectic.

"Guess what the idiots have done now," he shouted and the continued without waiting for my answer.

"A marketing group says they are willing to remove dead people from their mailing and telemarketing lists. What kind of yahoos are running businesses today?"

I didn't try to answer as I cut the strings on the bale of hay I was tossing to my horses.

"It says here," he shouted, "they have 5,200 members of this organization and they have decided to quit trying to sell stuff to dead people. They have even established a Do-Not-Contact list for the deceased. And to top it off, they are going to charge folks a dollar for every name they take off the list."

I looked up from my chores. He must have seen the puzzlement on my face, because he ranted on.

"They claim it is an effort to not disturb the families of people who are grieving. They must think everyone in the world just fell off a turnip truck. That's right, the world. These fools have members in the U.S. and 44 other countries."

I was still standing there with my mouth open when he started again.

"You better close your mouth. There's flies about, hoss. You'll be swallering one before you know it."

I shook my head in disbelief and headed for a chair in the back yard shade. He followed and sat down, took off his gimmee cap and wiped away a bead of sweat on his forehead. Our new puppy, Cody, came up to us wagging his tail. I reached down to pet him and Rags continued.

"Its almost more than a man can stand. The whole country is going to pot and nobody seems to have a handle on how to fix it. That pup has more sense than most folks in charge of things."

Still speechless, I slowly nodded in agreement. Cody is pretty smart.

"Well, if you ain't gonna say anything, I guess I'll go on about my business. I got to make sure my family has a dollar to stop those yokels from calling me after I die."

I nodded again, scratched Cody's tummy, watched Rags drive away, and thought about leaving a dollar and instructions for my family. I hate to hear the telephone ring now and I sure don't want to hear it ringing after I'm dead.

Don't Be an Idiot

There is a conspiracy, planned or unplanned, to make idiots of us all. Just listen to this. The government, the corporations, the media keep treating us as if we are a bunch of *stupidos* (that's Spanish for stupidos). Well, we may be idiots if we fit the description of what that term really means. It is a Greek word, *idiotes*, meaning people who may have a high IQ but are so self involved in themselves they focus entirely on their own lives and are ignorant of and, or uncaring about public affairs, concerns, events. You see, the problem is we are citizens of a nation for, by, and of the people and, as such, we hold the most important office in the land—private citizen.

I watch the news a lot. I am a news junky. I have been ever since my first days in broadcasting when I sat facing a microphone and reported local, national and international news.

Of course, these days I read newspapers from around the country thanks to the internet. I also watch the news on television, preferable the News Hour on PBS. Following that I watch the Daily Show with Jon Stewart on Comedy Central, not for the laughs but for truth that emerges in the midst of their satire.

Primarily, I read a lot "alternative" publications. I wrote for some of them for many years, so I have a soft spot in my heart for them. Those publications do not just accept the corporate and government news handouts at face value. They dig deeper and uncover some interesting truths.

I am not very swift sometimes, but I am informed. I just don't want to be an idiot. I hope some of you feel the way.

Drive-Thru Hay

When I got out of the army, I came home to rough stock rodeo and a great summer job: hauling hay. In those days they baler was pulled through the field where it scooped up the windrowed hay, swallowed, formed and tied bales and spit them out into the field. Lucky guys like me followed along in the sweltering June and July heat, bucking the bales up on the hay wagon. Then we hauled the hay to the farmer's barn, heaved it up into the second story hayloft and stacked it within. With our clothes soaked with sweat we, our skins covered with dirt and hay, our hands calloused by the hay hook, we earned our pay.

Today, when I run low on hay, I call my friends George and Tom and they deliver it to my barn, toss it into the loft and stack it, while I stand and watch. How is that for progress?

However, there is a new movement afoot in the land. Out in Wellington, Kansas, a farmer named Jerry Applegate came up with a peculiar approach to buying hay. He has "Hay-To-Go."

These bales are about one-third the size of a normal bale weighing eleven to eighteen pounds. They are string tied and shrink wrapped. A strap handle provides easy carrying and the wrap prevents the hay from getting on your clothes or your vehicle. This method also keeps the storage area free of dirt and hay.

You can get your Hay-To-Go in four different varieties—alfalfa, brome, prairie hay or straw. However, it ain't cheap. All this "convenience" comes at a hefty price ranging from $5 to $8 per bale. Hay-To-Go even has a web site. Doesn't everyone? It is www.haytogo.com.

I only have two questions. If you have animals that you feed hay to why would you be so particular about dust and dirt and hay leavings on your person, vehicle or barn? Question number two: How do you capture the leavings that follow the consumption of hay without encountering real dirt? Maybe someone will invent a Drive-Thru-Poop-Containing Unit. Rags Bandy and me are working on that. Meanwhile, check your cinch and ride on.

Ever Wonder

When Old Beans came by again the other day with one of those puzzled looks on his face, I poured him a cup of coffee and sat back and waited for the outburst.

He took a deep drink and said, "Ever wonder why the sun lightens our hair, but darkens our skin?"

I remarked that I hadn't given it much thought and he said, "That's the difference between you and me. I am a philosopher and you're not."

I just nodded.

"Ever wonder why women can't put on mascara with their mouth closed?"

"Ever wonder why psychics don't win the lottery?"

"Ever wonder why "abbreviated" is such a long word?"

"Ever wonder why doctors call what they do 'practice'?"

"That one," I said, "I have thought about."

"Yeah," Old Beans mused. "When are they going to get it right?"

I had one and I said quickly, "Ever wonder.why you have to click on "Start" to stop Windows 98?"

He just looked at with steely eyes and muttered, "Don't start on that computer stuff. I ain't interested. But, why is lemon juice made with artificial flavor, while dish washing liquid is made with real lemons?"

I filled his cup again, sat back, and wondered how long he had been thinking about all these things when he burst out with more.

"Ever wonder why the man who invests all your money is called a broker?"

"Ever wonder why there isn't dead mouse-flavored cat food?"

"Ever wonder who tastes dog food when it has a "new & improved" flavor?"

I jumped in with, "Why didn't Noah swat those two mosquitoes?"

He just harumped and said, That's an old one, hoss. But, have you ever wondered why they sterilize the needle for lethal injections? And why don't they make the whole plane out of the material used for the indestructible black box? And why sheep don't shrink when it rains?"

I was starting to get a headache as he paused for another long swig of coffee.

"Why do they call apartments when they are all stuck together? And if con is the opposite of pro, is Congress the opposite of progress?"

Now, that one caused me think a little. However, he was not finished.

"Why do they call the airport "the terminal" if flying is so safe? And just in case you need further proof that the human race is doomed because of stupidity, there are some actual label instructions on consumer goods that set my to spinning. On a Sears's hairdryer, it says 'Do not use while sleeping. Thunder, that's the only time I have to work on my hair. You know what it says on a bag of Fritos?"

I had to admit I had never read a bag of Fritos.

"That's a surprise," he said. "I thought you had read everything. Well, the other day on a bag of Fritos it said, 'You could be a winner! No purchase necessary. Details inside. And I thought this must be a shoplifter special. Then I read a bar of Dial soap: 'Directions: Use like regular soap.' And I thought 'and that would be how?"

I just sipped my coffee and smiled at him.

"You need to read more, hoss," he said. "On a Swanson frozen dinner it says, 'Serving suggestion: Defrost.' I thought well it's only a suggestion but what kind of eejit do they think I am. Then I read on the bottom of a Tesco's Tiramisu dessert 'Do not turn upside down. But, it was a mite too late.

"I got one!" I shouted and he nearly dropped his coffee cup.

"I saw on a package of Marks & Spencer Bread Pudding. It said, 'Product will be hot after heating" and I thought, well, duh!"

"You ain't so hopeless after all, are you," Old Beans said.

"But, I got a real winner for you. I bought a new iron the other day and on the packaging it said, 'Do not iron clothes on body.' You know what I thought? That would save me a lot of time. Then I read on a bottle of Boot's Children Cough Medicine:'Do not drive a car or operate machinery after taking this medication.' And I thought we could reduce construction accidents if we could just get those 5-year-olds with head-colds off those forklifts."

He paused before breathlessly continuing.

"On Nytol Sleep Aid it says: 'Warning: May cause drowsiness.'"

"On most brands of Christmas lights: 'For indoor or outdoor use only.' I'm thinking as opposed to ... what?"

"On a Japanese food processor: "Not to be used for the other use.""

"Now, Hoss, help me on this one. On Sunsbury's peanuts it says: "Warning: contains nuts." And on an American Airlines packet of nuts is says: "Instructions: Open packet, eat nuts." And how about this: On a child's superman costume it says: "Wearing of this garment does not enable you to fly." I don't blame the company. I blame the parents for this one.

On a Swedish chain saw I read:"Do not attempt to stop chain with your hands or.... genitals." Now, what's been going on there?'

With that, he shook his head, got up and left. I sat there in a daze trying to sort out what I had just heard.

Exam for the Aging

If you are over forty several things are happening. For instance, the battle of bulge joined by creeping memory loss. Therefore, I have a little exam to share with you.

1. After the Lone Ranger saved the day and rode off into the sunset, the grateful citizens would ask, "Who was that masked man?" Invariably, someone would answer, "I don't know, but he left this behind." "What did he leave behind?

2. When the Beatles first came to the U.S. in early 1964, we watch them on what show?

3. Complete this sentence: Get your kicks....

4. Complete this sentence: The story you are about to see is true. The names have been changed....

5. Complete this sentence: In the jungle, the mighty jungle ...

6. After the twist, the mashed potatoes, and the watusi, we "danced" under a stick that was lowered as low as we could go in a dance called what?

7. N_E_S_T_L_E_S, Nestle's makes the very best ... what?

8. Satchmo was America's "ambassador of goodwill." Our parents shared this great jazz trumpet player with us. His name was what?

9. What takes a licking and keeps on ticking?

10. Red Skelton's hobo character was whom?

11. Red Skelton always ended his television show by saying, "Good night, and...."

12. Some Americans who protested the Vietnam war did so by burning their....

13. The cute little car with the engine in the back and the trunk in the front, was the Volkswagen. What other names did it go by?

14. In 1971, singer Don MacLean sang a song about, "the day the music died." This was a tribute to whom?

15. The Russians put the first satellite into orbit. It was called what?

16. One of the big fads of the late 50's and 60's was a large plastic ring that we twirled around our waist; it was called it what?

The next page has the answers. How is your memory, old timers?

Answers:

1.   The Lone Ranger left behind a silver bullet.

2.   The Ed Sullivan Show.

3.   Route 66

4.   to protect the innocent.

5.   The Lion sleeps tonight.

6.   The limbo

7.   chocolate.

8.   Louis Armstrong

9.   The Timex watch.

10. Freddy the freeloader

11. Good night, and may God Bless."

12. draft cards (the bra was also burned)

13. Beetle or Bug

14. Buddy Holly

15. Sputnik

16. hoola-hoop

Fans

I know some folks are real fans of my column. However, I got a real surprise one day. And what a surprise! I have received fan letters from foreign countries like Australia and Arkansas.

It seems Dalzell Morris, an Australian member of the National Foundation Quarter Horse Association subscribes to the magazine, as well. My column has appeared in it for many years. Yep! There are horse people down under, you know. Remember "The Man from Snowy River?"

Dalzell looks forward to receiving the magazine over there in Australia and told the folks in Joseph, Oregon, where the magazine is published, "The journal is a must read when it arrives and Vernon Schmid's "Horse Sense" is my first read." He even said he clipped one recent column and pinned it to the wall by his telephone. That seems to me to be a little silly but I like thinking that the column is worth such a respected place on the wall.

I know sometime back an area veterinarian put a copy of one of my columns on the wall at the veterinarian hospital where he works. It was the one about vets and farriers always being late because they operate on God time. That is they do things when they get around to it.

At the dentist's to get my teeth cleaned, a dental technician stopped torturing me long enough to get an autograph. Now, that is just silly.

Well, that's enough about fans. But, I do thank them all and encourage them to check their cinches and ride on.

Feeling Groovy

Remember the old song lyrics, "Slow down you're going to fast. Got to make the morning last …" Well, on my recent trip out west, I sat on that Delta flight and that tune kept running through my head. I took it as a sign that I needed to slow down, needed to let the things that feel good take over my life. We often ignore things that make us feel good. Things like, "Falling in love." Not lust, real love. The kind of love that holds the world together.

And how about laughing so hard your face hurts, or a good hot shower after a hard day, and no lines at the supermarket. There are others, of course, and we need to need to embrace them all. A special glance from someone special in our lives, taking a drive on a pretty road, hearing your favorite song on the radio…. feeling groovy, or just getting mail. Lying in bed listening to the rain outside is a good feeling for me and hot towels fresh out of the dryer.

Milkshakes. Recently in Kansas I was really wanting a milkshake and my sister and niece and I were in a Braums ice cream joint and I ordered a 32 ounce milkshake. Why? Because I could. I couldn't finish it, but I sure tried even though my whole esophagus felt frozen. Ummm. Good.

Long distance phone calls from folks you really care about are nice. Giggling, good conversation, finding a $20 bill in your coat from last winter, and laughing at yourself are all groovy feelings.

Running through sprinklers, laughing for absolutely no reason at all, having someone tell you that you don't look as old as you really are, or laughing at an inside joke are also groovy.

I like real friends. You know the kind that you can just be yourself around. And, accidentally overhearing someone say something nice about you.

I got a long list including playing with a new puppy, new kitten, new baby, sweet dreams, hot chocolate, road trips with friends, and song lyrics printed inside your new CD so you can sing along without feeling stupid. At my age I still like making eye contact with a cute stranger. I also like seeing smiles and hearing laughter from friends, especially if I made them laugh. In addition, holding hands with someone you care about is right up there. I know its corny, but I like it.

Finally, I celebrate getting out of bed every morning and being grateful for another beautiful day to ride on.

First Nation's Know How

The native peoples of the Americas possessed skills and knowledge that eluded Europeans for hundreds, if not thousands of years. America's First Nations advanced their societies and improved the quality of their lives and ours before European engagement. As a participant in the celebration of the opening of the National Museum of the American Indian, I put together a list of contributions made by America's indigenous peoples.

Aztecs understood human anatomy long before Europeans possessed the knowledge. Indians used Coca, peyote and datura to ease pain, bacteria killing substances (yarrow, cranberries, maguey, salt) to prevent infections. They were sterilizing water by boiling it to clean wounds and incisions thousands of years before Europeans "discovered" the method in the early 20th Century. Treatments for illnesses were sometimes written in pictograms on bark as a prescription.

Aztecs kept their streets clean, established hospitals with physicians, nurses and pharmacists. People with contagious illnesses were often isolated (quarantined) to prevent spread of the disease, a practice not used by Western hospitals until the 20th Century. Indian physicians performed complex surgeries like draining fluid from the lungs and brain (survival rates were 50% as opposed to European rates of 10% at the time) and they used human hair as a suture. Aztec surgeons used obsidian scalpels for surgery including cataract surgery because they were sharper than anything else they possessed. Pre-contact Indians administered medicines under the skin with hypodermic syringes made from hollow bird's bones and small animal bladders. Europeans did not begin using syringes until 1835. Bathing often Indians used balsam and yucca root for shampoos and for cleaning clothing and other items. Jojoba was used as a hair conditioner. Aztecs used copal and balsam to neutralize body odor. Plains Indians stored sweet grass in their clothing. Indians cleaned their teeth often with a frayed stick. Aztecs polished their teeth with salt and charcoal. Salt water was used as a mouthwash. Sunflower oil, wallflower and aloe vera were used as sunscreen.

Food? How about this list, sunflowers, zucchini, corn, potatoes, avocados, pineapples, cashews, blueberries, vanilla, beans, sweet potatoes, popcorn, Bell and chili peppers, peanuts, navy beans, pumpkin, squash, maple and corn syrup, tomatoes, strawberries, black walnuts, herbs, chocolate, chewing gum (chicle, sweet gum, licorice root, and spruce sap).

Before the Europeans came Indians had ponchos, parkas, straight pins, umbrellas, irrigation, concrete, vulcanization, asphalt, suspension bridges, wet suits, copper pipes, plumbing, latex, dental inlays and fillings, compulsory education, camouflage, fishhooks, colanders, soldering, copper metallurgy, hockey, basketball, lacrosse, hammocks, disability rights, gold plating, metal foil, crop rotation, oil wells, adobe structures, fish fertilizer, forest and prairie management, carpentry techniques, a calculator developed by the Aztecs, astronomy with observatories and worship centers with windows aligned precisely to the rising and setting of the sun and Venus, books written by Toltecs, a working knowledge of geometry to build pyramids in about 3000 B.C. before the Egyptians built them.

For Lexophiles

Before you get on your high horse and start yelling at me about lexophiles you need to know that a lexophile is a person who loves words. And being one of those afflicted people I thought it my duty to share the following.

"A bicycle can't stand alone because it is two-tired."

"The definition of a will is a dead giveaway."

"Time flies like an arrow and fruit flies like a banana."

"A backward poet writes inverse."

"In democracy it's your vote that counts; In feudalism, it's your count that votes."

"A chicken crossing the road is poultry in motion."

"If you don't pay your exorcist you get repossessed."

"With her marriage she got a new name and a dress."

"Show me a piano falling down a mine shaft and I'll show you A-flat minor."

"When a clock is hungry it goes back four seconds."

"The man who fell into an upholstery machine is fully recovered."

"A grenade thrown into a kitchen in France results in Linoleum Blownapart."

"You feel stuck with your debt if you can't budge it."

"Local Area Network in Australia: the LAN down under."

"He often broke into song because he couldn't find the key."

"Every calendar's days are numbered."

"A lot of money is tainted. 'Taint yours and 'taint mine."

"A boiled egg in the morning is hard to beat."

"He had a photographic memory which was never developed."

"A plateau is a high form of flattery."

"The short fortuneteller who escaped from prison was a small medium at large."

"Those who get too big for their britches will be exposed in the end."

"When you've seen one shopping center you've seen a mall."

"Those who jump off a Paris bridge are in Seine."

"When an actress saw her first strands of gray hair she thought she'd dye."

"Bakers trade bread recipes on a knead to know basis."

"Santa's helpers are subordinate clauses."

"Acupuncture is a jab well done."

"Marathon runners with bad footwear suffer the agony of defeat."

Okay! So some are groaners. Check your cinch and groan on.

4-H

My own experience as a member of the 4-H was a long time ago. I raised a filly and a field corn as my projects. Both won prizes at the county fair. I never forgot the help and care I received from the sponsors. For those who are not in the know the 4-H is a non-formal educational, youth development program offered to individuals age 5 to 19.

These youth are involved in hands-on, experimental learning that allows learning by doing. All 4-H programs focus on active involvement and quality experiences, which stimulate lifelong learning of values and skills. I still remember the pledge. "I pledge my head to clearer thinking, my heart to greater loyalty, my hands to larger service and my health to better living, for my club, my community, my country and my world."

Now the creed is another matter. I had to look that up. My memory is not that good.

The creed goes like this: "I believe in 4-H Club work for the opportunity it will give me to become a useful citizen. I believe in the training of my HEAD for the power it will give me to think, plan and to reason. I believe in the training of my HEART for the nobleness it will give me to be kind, sympathetic and true. I believe in the training of my HANDS for the ability it will give me to helpful, skillful and useful. I believe in the training of my HEALTH for the strength it will give me to enjoy life, resist disease and to work efficiently. I believe in my country, my state and my community and in my responsibility for their development. In all these things I believe, and am willing to dedicate my efforts to their fulfillment."

That's a pretty good creed for all of us.

Fourth of July

When I was a boy the Fourth of July meant rodeos, the Star Spangled Banner sung badly, a small package of harmless firecrackers, a punk, too many hot dogs, ice cream, and when the sun began to set, sparklers. It was a big day for we rural types. Celebrating our nation's birth was an excuse to visit and race our horses and tell stories.

There wasn't any discussion about the founding of the nation. Politics weren't taboo, they just didn't seem important since President Roosevelt was lifting us out of the Great Depression and the dust bowl had worn itself out. Farmers and ranchers seem to have a new grasp on the future. It was a simple, albeit, naive time compared to today. Each year it brings me fond memories even as studies show the dumbing down of America.

Hey, we are who we are. Given a problem, we jump on our horses and ride at full gallop in every direction. Silly, but I like it better than the Canadian approach to issues, which comes off like "Now, now let's not get excited." Our approach is more fun. However, I like to celebrate with good folks and good memories. In the words of the poet Marianne Moore, "It is an honor to witness so much confusion."

Think about it! We are an odd group of people. Native Americans were nearly systematically eliminated and now the numbers increase each year. Black folk were humiliated, treated as chattel, and enslaved and yet they fought for and achieved the right to stand beside the rest of us in this polyglot nation and pursue their happiness. Chicanos (that's what they called themselves in my younger days) are now Latinos and growing in numbers and have become the largest minority group in the country. Then there are the Asians and Middle Easterners who come to this country, work hard and add to our rainbow of wonder. Even though our tolerance for diversity is nothing to brag about.

Still, we are an odd group. We put Elvis on a postage stamp even though some folk still believe he is alive. Some have seen flying saucers, believe in horoscopes (I used to write such a column when I was a newspaperman—I know how silly that is), palm readers, the lottery, and that you can get pregnant or AIDS from a toilet seat.

Look at our music: jazz, rock-a-billy, folk, Latino, pop, country, Salsa, baroque, Tejano, reggae, bluegrass, heavy metal, Cajun. I must have missed some, but you get the idea. All this says is that we are not a highly tasteful country and can do better than fast food joints and bobble-heads.

You get the idea. We are far from perfect, but there are millions of certified good folks out there and I wish them all many happy Fourths of July.

Freedom from Expectations

When I was in the seventh grade, my father decided to farm more land than our farm contained, so he rented some land down the road from our place. He planted it in wheat and just as the wheat was ripening the weather turned on him. He had only about two days to combine and store those many acres of wheat. He worked alone far into the night the first day, cutting the wheat, loading it into the truck, and hauling it to storage. However, it was clear that alone he would never beat the oncoming storm.

On the second day, he recruited help: my uncle fresh out of the army and my seventy pounds of skinny, freckled faced kid. His expectations were high for me and I worked hard and long into the night with dust filling my lungs and fatigue taking possession of every muscle in my body. However, we made it. We got the crop in and that night when we got home I could hardly walk. A small boy had done a man's job all day because his father expected it of him.

At home late that night my mother drew a bath, I climbed into it, and as soon as the water relaxed my aching body, I began to sob. The only word of compassion I heard was from my uncle, whom I heard from the other room say, "He did a man's job today."

A lot of spend our lives trying to live up to other's expectations. Yet, it is foolish and unnecessary to try to build our own worth on the expectations of another. It doesn't matter who it is: boss, wife, husband, mother, father, anyone who looks at what we do and decides we are not doing it right, or we should be doing more. Many of us carry this exhausting burden from childhood.

I like the Zen approach. Let things be as they are, check your cinch and ride on.

Getting Old and Laughing About It

One of my younger cousins, Charlie, is getting older and he thinks I'm ancient. He sent some jokes to me and for a change, some of them are funny, so here goes.

It seems an elderly well dressed, well groomed gentleman in a great looking suit with a flower in his lapel and smelling slightly of a good after shave walked into an upscale cocktail lounge. Seated at the bar is an elderly looking woman. He walks over, sits beside her, orders a drink, takes a sip, turns to her and says, "So tell me, do I come here often?"

Another elderly gentleman with serious hearing problems went to the doctor, the doctor fitted him with a set of hearing aids that allowed him to hear 100%.

The elderly gentleman went back in a month to the doctor and the doctor said, "Your hearing is perfect. Your family must be really pleased that you can hear again."

The gentleman replied, "Oh, I haven't told my family yet. I just sit around and listen to the conversations. I've changed my will three times!"

Two elderly gentlemen from a retirement center were sitting on a bench under a tree when one turns to the other and says … "Slim, I'm 83 years old now and I'm just full of aches and pains. I know you' re about my age. How do you feel?"

Slim says, "I feel just like a new-born baby."

"Really!? Like a new-born baby!?"

"Yep. No hair, no teeth, and I think I just wet my pants."

An elderly couple had dinner at another couple's house, and after eating, the wives left the table and went into the kitchen. The two men were talking, and one said, "Last night we went out to a new restaurant and it was really great. I would recommend it very highly."

The other man said, "What is the name of the restaurant?"

The first man thought and thought and finally said, "What is the name of that flower you give to someone you love? You know … the one that's red and has thorns."

"Do you mean a rose?"

"Yes, that's the one," replied the man. He then turned towards the kitchen and yelled, "Rose, what's the name of that restaurant we went to last night?"

Hospital regulations require a wheelchair for patients being discharged. However, one student nurse, found an elderly gentleman—already dressed and sitting on the bed with a suitcase at his feet—who insisted he didn't need help to leave the hospital. After a chat about rules being rules, he reluctantly let me wheel him to the elevator. On the way down, she asked him if his wife was meeting him.

"I don't know," he said. "She's still upstairs in the bathroom changing out of her hospital gown."

Goods Woods

An old farmhouse stands alone in a thicket of trees and brush. Over a hundred years ago, when the house was built from native limestone, the area was probably all prairies. A reminder of another time when hardy pioneers settled the region geologists call the Osage Questas, it is now a woodland area developed as part of the Kansas Wetlands and Riparian Areas Alliance.

While on book signing trip, I visited my friends Max and Eweleen Good on forty acres of recovering tall grass, woodland ponds and natural flora and fauna. Their home, built to blend with woodlands and prairie grasses, sits on the land purchased some thirty years ago. Max had been doing it all by himself. Then, about ten years ago, he learned of a federal program encouraging wetlands development. Working with a representative from the U.S. Fish and Wildlife Service, he plotted the area and received some government financing for the project.

"I've been working on this for 20 years," he told me. The entire acreage has been converted from cropland to native prairie and wetlands. It's home to 200 species of wildflowers, 55 species of vines and trees, 40 species of grasses and at least 200 species of birds, not to mention a host of other animals, from the five-lined skink to armadillos, bobcats, raccoons, coyotes, tree frogs, opossum, snakes, turtles, fish and deer.

Max admits the forty-acre site is small, but added, "What if everybody had 40 acres? Think how much wildlife you would have. It is amazing when you live here."

A commercial photographer, he has cameras with zoom lenses and a video camera set up on tripods by a picture window between his house and this wonder of recreated wilderness he has developed. He watches the critters in comfort and he and Eweleen are understandable excited by all they have done and seen.

It got me to thinking. With our farmland constantly eroded by housing developments and little being done to slow it down, where will our natural places be in twenty years? I still watch many varieties of birds through my kitchen window and we have a family of groundhogs living under garden shed, but it is a long way from "natural." The first year we lived here, I saw a fox loping along our fence line. I know there are raccoons around. They leave evidence in the garden. And of course, squirrels and rabbits. They are good at adapting. Nevertheless, I wish I could gaze across the property and see the land and the animals as they once were. Wouldn't that be a hoot?

Haying Time

Spring renews the earth. Long dormant flowering plants, fruit trees, and mysteries of nature thrust out flowering reminders that spring has arrived. For me there is another event that announcing spring. It is the slice and chop of the sickle laying low a field of hay that then awaits windrowing and the gobble, crush and tie of the baler. The smell of new mown hay is more exhilarating than any perfume.

In Kansas where I spent much of my boyhood there at least three cuttings a year, just as there is in Maryland. In the western high country, two cuttings suffice, usually in June and late August, depending on the water, or lack thereof. Nevertheless, haying time remains exciting, at least in my mind. At the same time that I am glad to just buy the hay for my horses and not have to cut and bale it myself, my lazy body encounters a restless memory that will not let me forget those days when neighbors moved from farm to farm to bale one another's hay, after each had mowed and windrowed.

The sprawling dinner tables (noontime in the country is dinnertime) were filled with every country dining delight from fried chicken to mounds of real mashed potatoes with gravy, vegetables fresh grown or canned from the year before, sauerkraut, relishes, and fresh baked bread with homemade butter and jams. Desert offered every imaginable kind of pie made from scratch. It is amazing to me today that those men could work after putting away all that food. Nevertheless, they did.

One summer really stands out in my memory. It was always hot in the summer, but that summer was especially hot. The temperature stood at 110 degrees Fahrenheit in the shade and, as my father remarked, "there ain't no shade." Still, they worked on and I faithfully carried ice water to them in the field although the ice would melt before I got there. Then, like something out of a scary movie, one of the men, a tough old farmer, collapsed. In those days, there was no 911. The others picked up out of the field and carried him into the shade of an old elm tree by the house. The women brought out cold, wet clothes to bath his face. They gave him sips of cool water, as he lay sprawled beneath the tree. The rest went back to the field. There was still work to be done. The hay had to be put up, before rain slipped into the sky and ruined it.

I continued to carry water to the field, my bibbed overalls soak with sweat. No, not perspiration, sweat! I kept one eye on the man in the shade of the tree. As he recovered, it was clear he felt humiliated. This was a time when men weren't supposed to cry, fold under pressure, or collapse when overheated. Finally, he got to his wobbly feet and went back to the field.

Haying time was a little tougher on the hayers in those days without air-conditioned tractor and baler cabs. However, the risk and the necessity to get it done was the same. Still, the smell of new mown hay announcing that summer is finally underway excites me. So, when spring comes check your cinch, lubricate your balers and ride on.

Health Care beyond the Norm

Like a lot of you, I have had a variety of injuries and health care issues over the years that physicians analyzed and threw drugs or surgery at the problem. That's alright sometimes. However, advanced age has led me to look at other means of physical and psychological maintenance.

Back when I surrendered to the fact that I had a hearing problem, I went to the veteran's administration for assistance. They checked me out and told me what Miss Susan and the daughters had been telling me for years. "Yup, you got a hearing problem." I told him to speak up, I had a hearing problem.

Then they sent me to a fellow who laid me down in the dark and then hooked all kinds of wires and doodads to my head. After a half-hour, he told me a sharp blow above my left ear caused the hearing loss. I said I always figured it was all those rock-a-billy gigs in the fifties and sixties. He said, "No."

The only sharp blow I could remember was the front hoof of a horse next to me who reared up in a parade and smacked me a good one when I was twelve. I told the specialist and he said enthusiastically, "Bingo!"

The bottom line to all this palaver is this: medical folks have come a long way. I even began to believe in chiropractic care back in the seventies. Massage therapy made a believer in me in the nineties. Then, I saw a Public Broadcasting special on the old Chinese healing art—acupuncture. That was followed by some reading and an encounter with Miss Susan's cousin back in Kansas—a chiropractor and licensed acupuncturist. So, one day I took the plunge.

I have had recurring severe lower back pain for nearly fifty years. I woke up with it and took it to bed with me at night. I always chalked it up to the bareback bronc riding days in the fifties. I told Rebecca, the acupuncturist, that was the problem. She said it wasn't physical. It was something else.

Now, I didn't just fall off the turnip truck. The opposite of physical is mental. And I can hear all the readers cheering and shouting, "He finally gets it. He's a mental case."

The acupuncturist explained that the kidneys are in your lower back and they are the center of your *chi*, the nerve center, if you will, of your physical existence. She said my problem was stress.

Now, I am impatient. Always have been. I set a goal and I want it accomplished now. My sleep for years has been interrupted by ideas, thoughts, and solutions taken to bed with me. Stress.

Once we talked about that aspect of my life, she invited me to take off my shirt and lie face down. I did. She calmly and quietly inserted tiny needles in selected locations along my spine. She left me alone to lay there and doze for a while. After about a half hour she came back into the room and removed the needles. She had me sit for a bit and drink some cold spring water. Then, I made another appointment and left to have dinner with my oldest daughter.

A short time later, standing outside the restaurant I suddenly realized I had no back pain. I can't wait until the next appointment.

I know. It doesn't sound like something an old cowboy type would do. But, hey, if it works....

Health Care Lies

Well, I did it. When my Methodist retirement health care plan required me to enroll in the new Medicare D prescription plan, I took a look at all the corporate insurance offered and sat in my chair stunned. The maze was nearly debilitating. And yet, it had to be done. So far, it has not saved me much money and it remains on ongoing nightmare.

My readers know that I am a reader and a researcher and fact gatherer. Therefore, I got some relief in learning that a couple in my age bracket, Anne and Dixie Leavitt, were completely bamboozled. They asked their son for help with the madness of the maze. He is a dutiful son, so he dropped by to help them find their way through the mess. The son is Michael Leavitt, Secretary of Health and Human Crevices and the head honcho and cheerleader for this healthcare nightmare created by the Bush Administration. Mike's daddy, Dixie, by the way, made his fortune in the insurance business and he couldn't figure out his son's own program.

The late President Dwight Eisenhower warned us about the military-industrial complex without knowing that an even bigger bug-a-boo looming on the horizon was the failing health care in the United States. The World Health Organization ranks the U.S. at 37th in health care. That puts us one notch ahead of Slovenia and below such national powerhouses as Malta, Columbia, Morocco, Chile and Dominica. Yeah, USA!

Our corporate health care is not only a nightmare for patients, pharmacists and physicians are inundated with mountains of paperwork and rules and regulations determining how they can treat their patients. What amazes me is that our health care is not an economic issue. We spend more money on health care than any other nation in history. It is not a health issue, either. We have the best physicians, nurses, technicians, nutritionists, and pharmacists in the world. Our heath care is a moral issue.

There are 46 million of our fellow citizens without health care. That is one in every six. There are 8.3 million children without health care. If you have been keeping score, and you should, you know that the numbers of uninsured have jumped by six million in the last five years. One-half of workers are paid less than

$20,000 annually and have no health insurance. Each year as many Americans die from lack of proper health as die from stroke, heart attacks, HIV or homicide all lumped together. Coupled with the fact that 29 million Americans are in medical debt and 70% of them had insurance. About a million of them file bankruptcy every year due to medical indebtedness and they are the ones with insurance.

Consumer drive health care programs guided and directed by pharmaceuticals and insurance lobbyists do not work. They have proven that repeatedly by failing. If we want to question the moral center of our nation the first place to look is at our health care. Martin Luther King, Jr. once said, "Of all the formed of inequality, injustice in health care is the most shocking and inhumane." That was decades ago and it has become worse.

That's my rant and now I'm off to see why my co-pays are getting higher every time I refill my prescriptions.

Health Tips

Old Beans Taylor had been thinking about health and longevity when he dropped by one morning for coffee. He said he had been reading. That was a little frightening because as anyone who knows Beans knows his reading habits can lead to some rather unique ideas.

"Did you know," he said. "That if you walk a lot it can add minutes to your life?"

"I heard that," I said.

"Well," he said. "I figure that if you do that live to be 85 years of age, you will be able to spend an additional five months in a nursing home at the cost of about $5000 per month. So, I'm not sure it's worth it."

"I see what you getting at," I replied.

"My old granny used to walk a lot," he said. "She started walking five miles a day when she was 60. Haven't seen her in years. We don't know where the hell she is."

"That's an old joke," I said.

"Ain't no joke when it's about one of your own."

"Do you exercise?" I asked.

"The only reason I would take up exercising is so that I could hear heavy breathing again. One of my nieces talked me into joining a health club last year. I spent about four hundred bucks. Didn't lose a pound. I guess you have to go there."

I just shook my head in disbelief as he dumped four spoonfuls of sugar into his coffee.

"If I exercised," he said. "I'd have to do it early in the morning before my brain figured out what I'm doing."

"Yeah, I know what you mean," I said. "We both came from a culture that believed if you couldn't do something from the back of horse it wasn't worth doing."

"Yup," he said. "Used to spend an hour getting a green broke horse ready to ride a hundreds."

"Well," I said. "I like long walks, especially when they are taken by people who annoy me."

"You got that right," he said. "My niece tells me I have flabby thighs, but I explained to her that is alright, since my stomach covers them."

"So, I guess the bottom line is that if you exercise every day you die healthier."

"I reckon," he said. "Meantime, I'm just gonna check my cinch and ride on."

High Country Thoughts

Driving through Colorado's upper Arkansas River Valley one summer, I got to thinking about how it was once the land of the Utes. Few other tribes dared venture into these mountains and high country valleys where the fierce Utes reigned supreme. The valleys and the high ridges around the mountains were filled with bison, elk, deer and antelope. It was good hunting for the Utes and added to their diet of trout, pinon nuts and various cactus concoctions it provided them with a good living.

Fur trappers like Kit Carson, Joe Meek, and others first explored this land. The pressure from whites who first wanted to mine the region for gold and silver displaced the Utes to only the western slope of the Rocky Mountains. Then it was the land itself beckoning ranchers and farmers. At an elevation of some 7,000 feet, Buena Vista, one town I lived in as a teenager, once was known for its lettuce production. Cattle still graze throughout the valleys. The Utes wound up on two small reservations in the southwest corner of the state and another in Utah.

My late sister, Margaret and her husband, Edward, a genuine Colorado native, lived on a small place near the foot of Poncha Pass. Nothing remarkable about that except their house was once a trading post that dealt with Ute allotments. Chief Ouray (The Arrow) and his mixed blood wife, Chipeta, were frequent visitors to the place, as was Chief Shavano.

I always stop and visit for a day or two when I am out that way. It gives me a break and I like the smell of pine and pinion that inundates the cool summer air where they live. And they are still true to the history of the place.

I used to ride the same trails the Utes and the trappers rode in the high country. My horse and I would pick our way carefully along trails that most folks had never seen back in the late forties. The trappers didn't get all the beaver because I have watched them work along Cottonwood Creek high in the mountains.

Today there are summer homes and flatland invaders everywhere it seems. Nevertheless, I still thrill to the memory of riding and camping where Kit Carson and the others were the first white men to see this magnificent place. These memories remind me that the past must be kept alive for us to know who we are today and from where we have come. It is true here, as well. As developments gobble up farm land and people fill the houses where once only the land existed, it behooves us to remember where we have been so we know how we got to where we are. Meanwhile, ride on.

How Did We Make It?

Rags was fussing when we met for coffee the other morning.

He said, "I can't believe we made it."

"How's that? I said.

"Well," he continued, "You know when we were kids we rode in cars with no seat belts or air bags and riding in the back of a pick-em-up truck on a warm day was always a special treat."

"Yeah," I said. "Folks are really safety conscious today."

"Our baby cribs were covered with bright colored lead-based paint to say nothing of our window and door sills," he said. "And we didn't eat the paint."

"Wonder why?" I asked.

"Our folks taught us not to graze on the woodwork."

"I guess so. And you know we had no childproof lids on medicine bottles, doors, or cabinets, and when we rode our bikes, we had no helmets. Heck, we even hitchhiked to town as a young kid!"

"Remember drinking water from the garden hose and not from a bottle?" he asked.

"I remember when you and I rode a homemade sled down a hill into the blackberry briars three times before we decided it wasn't a very smart thing to do," I said with a grin.

"We didn't have curfews," he said. "When we didn't have work to do we could leave home and play all day, as long as we were back when the kerosene light was lit in the kitchen. Sometimes, no one was able to reach us all day. No cell phones. Unthinkable for young'ns today. They don't want to be out of touch for a minute. The truth is they are already out of touch with reality with that thing stuck in their ear all day."

"We got cut up and broke bones and broke teeth, and there were no law suits from these accidents. They were accidents. No one was to blame, but us. Remember accidents?"

"Yeah, we had fights and punched each other and got black and blue and learned to get over it."

"Remember what we ate," I added.

147

"Yeah," Rags said. "We ate pork and lots of it, homemade cookies and cupcakes, bread and butter, and drank sugar soda when we could get it but we were never overweight because when we weren't working we were outside playing. We shared one grape soda with four friends, from one bottle and no one died from it."

"How did we ever make it?"

Rags smiled and sipped his coffee.

"We had friends. That's how we got by. We rode bikes or walked or rode a horse to a friend's home. Imagine such a thing. Without asking a parent! By ourselves! Out there in the cold cruel world! Without a guardian. How did we do it?"

"And we made up games with sticks and corncobs and ate worms and although we were told it would happen we did not put out very many eyes, nor did the worms live inside us forever."

"I even remember when 4-H was hard and in high school the Future Farmers of America sponsor was your high school shop teacher. He had you coming and going. Not everyone was best at everything and when you weren't you learned to deal with disappointment without your parents threatening to sue somebody."

"Or sending you to a therapist."

"And some students just weren't as smart as others so they failed a grade and were held back to repeat the same grade and tests were not adjusted for any reason? In fact, I knew a boy who was the only eighth grader who drove himself to school in his own car."

"I think it was because we knew about consequences."

"Yep," Rags said as he waved the waitress over to freshen our coffee. "Our actions were our own. Consequences were expected. There was no one to hide behind. The idea of a parent bailing us out if we broke a law was unheard of. They actually sided with the law, or our teachers, imagine that!"

"Our generation produced some of the best risk-takers and problem solvers and inventors, ever. We had freedom, failure, success and responsibility, and we learned how to deal with it all."

"Yeah," Rags grinned. "We're part of that bunch. Congratulations, Vern!"

"Right back at you!"

How to Bath a Cat

In this era of overly political correctness, I know this will offend some folks, including my older daughter who has two beautiful Maine Coon cats. However, I have been offending folks for a long time, so why stop now. You see I was talking to my new pup, Cody, the other day. He had some instructions for me regarding cats and how to bath them. It went something like this:

1. Thoroughly clean the toilet.

2. Add the required amount of shampoo to the toilet water, and have both lids lifted.

3. Obtain the cat and soothe him while you carry him towards the bathroom.

4. In one smooth movement, put the cat in the toilet and close both lids (you may need to stand on the lid so that he cannot escape). CAUTION: Do not get any part of your body too close to the edge, as his paws will be reaching out for any thing they can find. The cat will self-agitate and make ample suds. Never mind noises coming from your toilet, the cat is actually enjoying this.

5. Flush the toilet three or four times. This provides a "powerwash" and rinse."

6. Have someone open the door to the outside and ensure that there are no people between the toilet and the outside door.

7. Stand behind the toilet as far as you can, and quickly lift both lids.

8. The now-clean cat will rocket out of the toilet, and run outside where he will dry himself.

Well, when Cody was finished telling me all of this I reminded him that his barking during my naptime in the afternoon was a real nuisance and that he hadn't been bathed in a while. As I led him toward the bathroom, he began to whine about how soap gets in his eyes and he really doesn't care for cold baths. And, he insisted the "powerwash" idea was one he had picked up from the neighbor's dogs.

How to Kill Time at Wal-Mart

Some of my friends are pretty sick puppies. However, they do come up with funny things now and then. To my advantage, they send them on to me and I adapt some of them for use in my column. These things to do at Wal-Mart while your spouse takes her sweet time delighted me.

- Get 24 boxes of condoms and randomly put them in people's carts when they aren't looking.
- Set all the alarm clocks in house wares to go off at 5-minute intervals.
- Make a trail of tomato juice on the floor leading to the rest rooms.
- Walk up to an employee and tell him or her in an official tone, 'Code 3' in house wares.... . and see what happens.
- Go the Service Desk and ask to put a bag of M&M's on lay away.
- Move a 'CAUTION—WET FLOOR' sign to a carpeted area.
- Set up a tent in the camping department and tell other shoppers you'll invite them in if they'll bring pillows from the bedding department.
- When a clerk asks if they can help you, begin to cry and ask 'Why can't you people just leave me alone?'
- Look into the security camera; use it as a mirror, and pick your nose.
- While handling guns in the hunting department, ask the clerk if he knows where you can find the anti-depressants.
- Dart around the store suspiciously loudly humming the "Mission Impossible" theme.
- Hide in a clothing rack and when people browse through, say "PICK ME! PICK ME!"
- When an announcement comes over the loud speaker, fall down, assume the fetal position and scream "NO! NO! It's those voices again!!!!"

- And last but not least!—Go into a fitting room and shut the door and wait a while; and, then, yell, very loudly, "There is no toilet paper in here!"

- Finally, check your cinch, ride on, and don't tell Wal-Mart managers where you got these ideas.

If I Were a Truck

If I were a truck, I would be thinking about trading in my body for a newer model about now. I have bumps, dents, and scratches in my finish and my paint job is getting a little dull, but that's not the worst of it.

My fenders are too wide to be considered stylish. They were once as sleek as a little MG I owned; now they look more like an old beat-up Buick I traded in long ago. My seat cushions have split open at the seams and are my seats are sagging. Seat belts? I almost gave up all belts when a new Mexican restaurant opened my neighborhood!

Air bag's? Forget it. The only bags I have these days are under my eyes. That's not counting the saddlebags around my waist, of course.

My old pick-em-up truck has nearly 200,000 miles on it, but I have so many miles on my odometer that the sucker is broken. Sure, I have been many places and seen many things, but when is the last time an appraiser factored life experiences against depreciation?

I have had laser surgery for cataracts, but my headlights are still out of focus and it's especially hard to see things up close, and far away. They took out part of a lung twenty years ago so my air filter doesn't work anything like it did fifty years ago.

Traction? My traction never was very graceful, but its worse these days. I slip, slide, skid, and bump into things even in the best of weather. And when there is ice on the ground I am an accident waiting to happen. My mechanics are a physician, chiropractor, massage therapist and acupuncturist who try their darnedest to keep me moving, but it is challenge. I feel sorry for those folks every time I keep an appointment with them.

My whitewalls are stained with varicose veins and it takes me hours to reach my maximum speed. To top all that off my fuel rate burns inefficiently. I once could run for hours on a good bowl of chili red. Now, I not only have gas but my body belches acid. But here's the worst of it—almost every time I sneeze, cough or sputter.... .either my radiator leaks or my exhaust backfires.

Just Call It Like You See It

Rags Bandy went to his physician the other day complaining that his ears were ringing, he throat felt like it was closing up on him, and his eyes felt like they were about to pop out. Doc looked him over and had him say "Aww" and then said, "You're tonsils will have to come out."

So, Rags went to the hospital and they ripped his tonsils out. He got over that and realized he still felt the same way. So, his doctor said, "I think what you really need is inner-ear surgery." So Rags went back into the hospital and they performed the operation and sent him to recover. He was getting well and one day noticed that all the symptoms were back. So, this time he decided to go to the big city and see a specialist.

He got into the big city and met with this over-priced specialist who examined him and said, "Mr. Bandy, I'm afraid you have a terminal illness. There is nothing I can do for you."

"How long do I have, Doc?" Rags asked.

"I'd say about six months," the specialist said.

Rags was really distraught. He went home and began putting his affairs in order. And decided he needed to get a new clothes, so he would look good at his funeral. He went to the county seat and stopped in at a men's clothing store. The clerk measured him for his new suit of clothes. The clerk said, "Thirty-four inch sleeves, thirty-two inch inseam, forty inch waist, sixteen inch collar."

"Wait just a dang minute," Rags said. "I wear a fifteen inch collar. Always have."

The clerk looked at him and said," Sir, if you wear a fifteen inch collar you throat will feel constricted, your ears will ring, and your eyes will bulge out."

Just Talkin'

Well, they came by again and Rags and Old Beans were in their best form.

They remind me of the saying, "Talk is cheap because supply exceeds demand." They also remind me of the adage "Age doesn't always bring wisdom. Sometimes age comes alone." But, I also know that you don't stop laughing because you grow old, you grow old because you stopped laughing.

So, I settled in while they got a cup of coffee and sat down on the back porch and started whittling. I got them soft whine pine so they wouldn't whittle on the porch itself. Rags kicked it off.

"Heard a good one the other day," he said. "Love is grand; divorce is a hundred grand."

Old Beans hee-hawed a while about that and then began musing about all the folks concerned about nutrition and working so hard to keep in physical shape.

"I don't know what all the fuss is about," he said. "There is no question that I am a nutritional overachiever, but I'm in shape. Round is a shape, ain't it?"

Well, I plan on living forever. I want to do everything I can to stay alive," I said.

Old Beans looked me over real careful and muttered, "So far, so good."

"I want to know what all the fuss is about professional contractor and them having to be licensed and bonded," Rags said. "You know amateurs built the ark. Professionals built the Titantic."

"And what about them politicians up in Washington," Old Beans said. "Ain't they something to behold?"

"Shoot," Rags said. "You know politicians and diapers have one thing in common. They should both be changed regularly and for the same reason."

"Somebody ought to tell them," Old Beans said, "That even if you are on the right track, you'll get run over if you just sit there."

They were quiet for a while and then Old Beans said, "You know, I been thinking a lot and I've come to the point where I believe a day without sunshine is just like night."

Rags looked at him open-mouthed for a long time and then just shook his head as he said, "It's frustrating when you know all the answers, but nobody bothers to ask you the questions."

"Amen," I said. "Check your cinch and ride on."

Landmarks

When traveling landmarks are important. They are especially important if you get off the interstate and drive through unfamiliar territory. As a boy in Colorado, I used mountains, creek and rivers, beaver dams, rocks and things like that. Living in Kansas, we were lucky enough to have most of the state crisscrossed with roads about every mile. If you missed a turn off you were only a mile off. Moving east confused us. Highways marked north and south had no relationship to those directions, so Miss Susan and I got lost a lot in those early years back in 1970s.

I still get turned around a bit when my western trained mind takes over. Recently I took Miss Susan out for dinner in Oxford, Pennsylvania, and when we left, I thought I would just take a turn around through town and take a look-see. It was getting dark so we drove along the highway and suddenly we were out of town. To make matters worse it was a moonless night and dark as pitch and I could not see a thing. I kept reassuring her that there would be a turn off somewhere ahead. There wasn't. Then I noticed the fuel gauge signaling that it was all about over.

Now I had two tanks on my old pick-em-up-truck. Therefore, I switched tanks and the gauge told me to just forget it. There was no fuel in the other one either. I put on a brave face and told Miss Susan that since we were on a highway there had to be a service station somewhere ahead of us along the road. There wasn't. I kept driving. Then we entered a town and it began to look familiar. I saw some landmarks, found a station, filled up both tanks, did a little shopping and headed home.

I thought that was a bizarre episode until I heard the story of a preacher's wife who moved from West Virginia to the Delmarva Peninsula as a newly wed. She kept memorizing landmarks as she tried to learn her way around the area. Finally, one day she went on an errand by herself and got lost. She got home later than expected and when the preacher asked why she got lost, she said they moved the sign.

What sign, he wanted to know. She told him it was the Argo 222 sign.

It seems the farmer harvested his crop and removed the seed sign. With the landmark gone, she got lost.

By the way, she asked me not to repeat this story. However, it makes my getting lost not seem so silly. Sorry, Ramona.

Language Lessons

My old friend Rags enlightened me one day about the George W. Bush administration in Washington, D.C. He sat on the back porch with me and ruminated about a whole new language permeating the executive branch.

"What do you mean?" I asked. "Aren't they just another team of double-talking bureaucrats?"

"Nope," he said. "You got it all wrong. There's a whole new language running around up there."

"Like what?"

"Well, young George brought a lot of pals from Texas and folks not born out in cowboy country may think they talk funny."

"Like you and me," I said.

"Yep. If I said the pickup engine's runnin' but ain't nobody driving, what would you think I meant?"

"Not overly-intelligent?" I offered.

"You got it. Here's a test for you, perfessor. As welcome as a skunk at a lawn party means what?"

"Well, that's sort of explanatory."

"Okay. How about "tighter than bark on a tree."

"Not very generous."

"Right. Big hat, no cattle."

"All talk and no action?"

"You doing good, Vern. Now how about 'We've howdied but we ain't shook yet.'"

"I think that means 'we've made a brief acquaintance, but not been formally introduced.'"

"You got it, Hoss. I like to use that one that goes 'He thinks the sun come up just to hear him crow.'"

"That means 'He has a pretty high opinion of himself, doesn't it?"

"It do. Ever hear 'She's got tongue enough for 10 rows of teeth?'"

"Yes. That usually means That woman can sure talk."

"There's a lot more of them," Rags said.

"My daddy used to say, 'It's so dry the trees are bribin' the dogs' every time we were short of rain."

"Mine used to say, 'Just because a chicken has wings doesn't mean it can fly' which meant appearances can be deceptive."

"Well, Rags," I offered, "How do you feel about all the new goings on in Washington?"

"Well, I'll tell you, this ain't my first rodeo. I've been around awhile and things come and go, but not much changes in the long run."

"Ever hear any really hard put-downs?"

"Yeah," Rags grinned. "I always liked the one 'He looks like the dog's been keepin' him under the porch.'"

"That's ugly," I offered. "How about the one that goes 'those sinners out there that been eating supper before they say grace.'"

Rags grinned. "Ever have anybody tell you that it was time to paint your rear white and run with the antelope? That's what my daddy used to tell me when I argued instead of doing what I was told. And if my daddy was around he would look at those folks in Washington and say, "You can put your boots in the oven, but that doesn't make them biscuits."

Legal Stills

Miss Susan and I were having lunch with her farmer Uncle Leon and Aunt Dorothy in Garnett, a little town in east-central Kansas. After a nice lunch, they took us on a drive around the new ethanol plant near town. We had already encountered excitement among Kansas farmers when we visited with her farmer brother Bill and his wife, Mona. They use ethanol in their vehicles and are as excited as any new converts about the product.

Ethanol has three positive aspects. One, it is good fuel and two; it is a market for corn producers; three, it doesn't harm the environment (no harmful exhaust emissions from vehicles including greenhouse gas emissions). Uncle Leon noted that huge trucks filled with shelled corn arrive regularly at the plant where they process it into ethanol, a colorless liquid with an agreeable odor that comes from distillation.

They have been making ethanol since ancient times with the fermentation of sugars. You folks with stills and bootleggers in your family history know all about the process. All beverage ethanol and more than half of industrial ethanol continues to be made by the same process. The fermentation reaction is complex and impure cultures of yeast produce varying amounts of other substances, including glycerin and various organic acids.

Used as an automotive fuel it is mixed with gasoline to form gasohol or used alone to fuel automobiles. Produced from various biomass materials such as corn, potato, cheese whey, paper sludge and wood waste, its primary base product these days is corn. When used as a transportation fuel, ethanol is referred to as E85, which is an alcohol fuel comprised of 85% ethanol and 15% gasoline. Additionally, studies have shown that the production and use of ethanol adds value to local farmer's crops and strengthens the local economy. Due to government subsidies, E85 is generally slightly cheaper than regular 87-octane gasoline.

So, what cars can use E85? Since 1996 Chrysler, Ford, and General Motors have manufactured and sold over 1.6 million flexible fuel vehicles (FFVs) nationwide that are capable of operating on E85 fuel or conventional gasoline. Most drivers of these vehicles are unaware of the flexible fuel nature of their vehicles. If you drive one, try E85!

By the way, the Kansas Legislature recently passed a bill rescinding a former law requiring service stations to label their fuel if they sold ethanol in their pumps.

And guess what else is on the horizon, my farmer friends, soy diesel.

Lessons Learned from Tippy

When Miss Susan and I married some thirty years ago, she received something in the contract for which she didn't bargain. It was my aging black Labrador Retriever. He was a genius dog. He didn't do much around the house, but he loved the outdoors. And he taught me a lot about how we humans could enjoy a fruitful and good life. I share the lessons with you now.

1. Never pass up the opportunity to go for a joy ride.
2. Allow the experience of fresh air and the wind in your face to be pure ecstasy.
3. When loved ones come home, always run to greet them.
4. When it is in your best interest, practice obedience.
5. Let others know when they have invaded your territory.
6. Take a lot of naps and stretch before rising.
7. Run, romp, and play every day.
8. Eat with gusto. Stop when you have had enough.
9. Be loyal.
10. Never pretend to be something you are not.
11. If what you want lies buried, dig until you find it.
12. When someone is having a bad day, be silent, sit close by and nuzzle them gently.
13. Thrive on attention and let people touch you.
14. Avoid biting when a simple growl will do.
15. On warm days, stop to lie on your back in the grass, and wiggle.
16. On hot days, drink lots of water and lay under a shade tree.

17. When you are happy, dance around and wag your entire body.

18. No matter how often you are scolded, don't buy into the guilt thing and pout—run right back and make up.

19. Delight in the simple joy of a long walk.

Thanks Tippy.

Libraries and Librarians

I have haunted of libraries all my life. It was regular weekly stop when I was a boy on the farm in Kansas. Miss Susan works in a library and she brought me a collection of thoughts about libraries and librarians.

One is a stern commandment attributed to a monastery in Barcelona, Spain. It says: "For him that stealeth a book from this library, let it change into a serpent in his hand and rend him. Let him be struck by palsy and all his members blasted. Let him languish in pain, crying aloud for mercy, and let there be no surcease for his agony until he sink to dissolution. Let bookworms gnaw his entrails in token of the worm that dieth not, and when at last he goeth to his final punishment let the flames of hell consume him for ever and ever."

Michael Moore once said, "I really didn't realize the librarians were, you know, such a dangerous group…. You think they are just sitting at the desk, all quiet and everything. They are like plotting the revolution, man. I wouldn't mess with them. You know, they've had their budgets cut. They're paid nothing. Books are falling apart. The libraries are just like the back end of everything."

Another observer of librarians, Will Manley wrote in his book *The Truth About Reference Librarians*, "a few simple mathematical calculations reveal that if reference librarians were paid at market rates for all the roles they play, they would have salaries well over $200,000."

Garrison Keiller in *Lives of the Cowboys* wrote, "Librarians, Dusty, possess a vast store of politeness. These are people who get asked regularly the dumbest questions on God's green earth. These people tolerate every kind of crank and eccentric and mouth breather there is."

The character Spider Robinson in the book *The Callahan Touch* said, "Mary Kay is one of the secret masters of the world: a librarian. They control information. Don't ever tick one off."

James Quinn said, "Our whole American way of life is a great war of ideas, and librarians are the arms dealers selling weapons to both sides."

"You honor your reservations; you go to your meetings so we can clean the rooms; you're relatively quiet; and you drink more than the American Legion."

So, said an anonymous hotel official, on why he liked the American Library Association annual conference.

Finally, a thought from David Sawyer. "Blaming the library for exposure to pornography is like blaming the lake if your child walks up to it alone, falls in and then drowns."

Like the Back of My Hand

As the New Year rolled around, I flew into the Kansas City, Missouri airport, drove south to my old Kansas home town, gathered up my gray-haired baby sister, Barbara, and we took to the road for two days in an Alamo rental car.

We visited the little town of Sedan, Kansas, where a fancy quilt shop operates. My sister is a quilter, so the trip was really for her benefit. All I know about quilts is that they keep you warm. Most memorable to me was getting lost going to Sedan.

Sedan is sixty miles west of the place where I was born and raised. It is just off U.S. 166. I took U.S. 160 west. My baby sister kept mumbling something like "This doesn't look familiar to me" and "I think we may have taken a wrong turn."

I kept assuring her I knew the country like the back of my hand. It became obvious I had not looked at the back of my hand for a while when we reached Elk City, Kansas, in the heart of the Flint Hills. She called her daughter Jackie. Being an intelligent young woman Jackie asked, "Don't you have a map?" The answer was obvious. No! The rental car agent tried to give me one but I assured him I knew the area "Like the back of my hand."

My laughing niece cranked up her computer and told us how to get back on U.S. 166. We visited Sedan and then left for Tahlequah, Oklahoma. We followed U.S. 166 east and I turned and headed south. Oklahoma, for all you eastern folks, is south of Kansas. I know the area like the back of my hand.

We drove around a bit, my sister needed a pit stop, and I needed to get directions. The back of my hand did not look familiar anymore. We stopped at a convenience store in Quapaw, Oklahoma. Quapaw is famous for two things: The U.S. government moved the Quapaw Indians there during the great removal and it has a casino.

Sister headed for the restroom and I looked a rack of maps. There were no maps of Oklahoma for sale. Stunned I asked the two employees, their boss, and a couple of customers if they knew the quickest way to Tahlequah.

You know that look a deer has when it stands in the road blinded by the headlights of your car. They had that look. They said nothing. Then, one of the customers suggested I go east into Missouri, head south to Siloam Springs, Arkansas, and then west into Oklahoma. She said that might get me there. Now, I may have fallen off a turnip truck but it wasn't yesterday. I know Oklahoma like the back of my hand.

Sister and I got back in the car and I headed south. It didn't matter what highway I was on. I knew Tahlequah was south. At lunchtime, we stopped at a small cafe to eat. We were discussing the fact that I knew the country like the back of my hand when a waitress overheard us and said, "Just go a block east of here and head south. You'll see signs directing you to Tahlequah. It's simple."

I took a bite of my hot beef sandwich and said to me sister, "See. I told you I know this country like the back of my hand." She is still giggling.

Lonesome Charley

Lonesome Charley was an unlikely candidate to be a frontier scout. He was born March 20, 1842 in Warren County, Illinois. Christened Charles Alexander Reynolds, he was the son of a physician who moved with his family to Kansas while Charley was in his teens. The baby faced young man attended Abingdon College. With the Civil War erupting, he left college in 1860 to join the Union Army as a volunteer.

He rarely drank, or smoked. Girls made him blush. He picked up the nickname "Lonesome" after his wartime service because he drifted from state to state and job to job and kept his private life very private. By 1865, he was a trader, but a year later, he was hunting buffalo on the high plains. In 1867, he and an Army officer at Ft. McPherson quarreled resulting in a fight in which the officer was injured and lost an arm.

Lonesome Charley hurriedly left that area and by 1869 was earning his living as a hunter and guide. He was good at his profession. His skill with a rifle led the Indians to call him *Hunter-Who-Never-Goes-Out-For-Nothing*.

It was as a hunter and guide that he encountered Lieutenant Colonel George Armstrong Custer, who convinced Charley to join him as chief scout for the Seventh U.S. Cavalry. Shortly he was earning his $100 per month pay as Custer led his expeditionary force into the Black Hills in direct violation of the treaty signed at Ft. Laramie in 1868. The expedition discovered what they were looking for—gold.

Assigned to take the news to Ft. Laramie, Lonesome Charley cleaned his rifle, filled his saddlebags with hardtack and cooked bacon, filled his ammunition belt, collected his canvas dispatch bag and was soon ready to ride.

He selected a horse from the troops' remuda, an animal so spirited it was considered unfit for regular cavalry use and began the long hot and Indian infested 120-mile journey. The horse was just what he needed to get him through to Fort Laramie in one piece with his hair still attached.

When Charley picked up the bag, he noticed that the expedition adjutant, Lieutenant James Calhoun, Custer's brother-in-law, had labeled the bag: *Black Hills Express Charley Reynolds, Manager Connecting with All Points East, West,*

North, South Cheap Rates, Quick Transit; Safe Passage We are protected by the Seventh Cavalry!

The Seventh Cavalry did ride with Charley part of the way. They escorted him to the edge of the Black Hills. They bivouacking near the South Fork of the Cheyenne River and about midnight, Custer shook Reynolds's hand and the scout rode off by himself into the darkness.

Before the sunrise, Charley was camped along a trickle of a stream. He holed up throughout the hot day and traveled by night. This lessened the chance of clashing with Indians. Water was scarce and he was forced to move around on hands and knees to gather enough dry grass to feed his horse.

On August 8, five days after leaving Custer at the edge of the Black Hills, Reynolds rode into Fort Laramie and turned Custer's dispatches over to an Army telegraph operator. Soon the word spread that gold was discovered in the Black Hills. However, that was not the end of Charlie's trip.

In addition to Custer's dispatches, Lonesome Charley carried a small bundle of private mail from the soldiers of the Seventh Cavalry. From the fort, he took a stagecoach to Cheyenne, some 90 miles to the south. At Cheyenne, he boarded a Union Pacific train, delivered the mail to a railway clerk and rode to Omaha, 516 miles to the east. Then he went back north by train to Bismarck. Lonesome Charley arrived at Fort Abraham Lincoln on August 19, just 16 days after he had left the Black Hills. Praised for his resolute sense of duty in carrying out his assignment he trained with the Seventh and tied his future to bigger things to come in 1876 at a place the Plains Indians called Greasy Grass.

The night before the historic battle, he had premonitions and gave away his personal items to the soldiers. As they were riding toward the Indian village prior to the battle, Charlie, who never drank, said he had never felt so discouraged or depressed in his life. He then asked interpreter Fred Gerard for some whiskey.

During the battle, he was killed. His body was buried on the battlefield and his grave crudely marked. Later, as with all of Custer's slain soldiers and civilians, a white marble slab marked the spot where he fell. Then his remains, like those of his comrades, were reentered on Custer Hill with an obelisk to commemorate their deaths.

Looking for Mister Button

Some years ago, I had student in one of my college classes who was older than the others were. A Vietnam vet, his dark eyes would twinkle when one of my jokes sailed right over the other younger students' heads. He got it. We were in harmony.

We served on a committee at the college planning for a Native American Day celebration. He was called "Wolf." His Anglo name was Wilbur Button. I liked him and when his health worsened and he had leave school, I missed him.

One day at the college, we were talking about origins and I mentioned that scientific types have traced the first residents of this continent back about 25,000 years. He smiled, his indigenous eyes sparkled and he said, "Some of us believe we have always been here.

I thought, "Yeah!"

I saw him some time later in an area shopping mall and he introduced me to his wife as "Dr. Schmid, the German Indian."

It was a long time after that when I saw a hawk swooping across the sky at my place and I thought of him. I wanted to find him just to visit, have a cup of coffee, maybe a snack and talk—or be silent. It would be good either way.

I wanted to tell him that since our last meeting my genealogical research has uncovered a Cherokee link. So, maybe the "German Indian has found his place among American Indians. At least I knew my identification with Indian causes has roots.

So, I went looking again, mentioned seeing the hawk and wondering about him in one of my columns.

A few days later, his wife called and said, "You should know Wolf died. He told me to watch the sky and if I saw a hawk, that would be him."

I watch the sky.

Marital Bliss

Rags Bandy and Beans Taylor came by the other day and we got to talking about our wives. Old Beans said he heard about a man who married a woman from Colorado and told her on their wedding night she was expected to do the dishes and keep the house clean.

"And how did that go?" Rags asked.

"Well," Beans said, "It seemed it took a couple days, but on the third day he came home to a clean house and the dishes were washed and put away.

Rags said he heard about another man who married a woman from Nebraska and told her essentially the same thing although he waited until the day after the wedding.

"Did she do it?" I asked.

"The first day there was no change," Rags said. "And the second day he noticed that the all the cleaning, dishes, and cooking wasn't quite up to snuff. But by the third day, the house was clean, the dishes were done, and there was a huge dinner on the table.

"I don't believe it," I said.

"Sounds like some kind of coffee shop lie," Rags said.

Beans said he was positive the stories were true and when he heard them, he told his wife things had to change. He said he laid the law down to her and told her she had to start keeping the house cleaned, dishes washed, lawn mowed, laundry washed and hot meals on the table for every meal.

"Did it work?" Rags asked.

"Yup," Old Beans said. "The first day I didn't see anything, the second day I didn't see anything, but by the third day some of the swelling had gone down and I could see a little out of my left eye, just enough to fix myself a bite to eat and load the dishwasher.

Nascar Challenged

Except for a horse running flat out across the prairie or on a racetrack, I have never cared much for speed. Even as a teenager, fast cars did not impress me. In fact, when a friend asked me along for a ride down the twisting U.S. 50 highway from Salida to Canon City, Colorado, late one night, I accepted knowing my life was all but over. He drove so fast around curves with a cliff on one side and the Arkansas River on the other I became convinced ours was an involuntary suicide mission.

Therefore, it came as no surprise when I went into a Home Depot out west to buy a gift card for a newly wed couple. My brother-in-law directed me to the proper counter. The smiling young clerk was very helpful until she came to selecting the artwork on the card.

"Would they like flowers?" she asked.

I had no idea.

"How about one with special construction designs on it?

I shrugged.

"We have others," she seemed to be getting impatient as she laid several on the counter top. "You pick the design and we'll credit the card for them."

I stood there like a dummy torn between all the choices. I hate that. I hate it when restaurants and all those other places make you choose. Finally, she broke the silence.

"How about a Tony Stewart?" she asked.

I was bumfuzzled.

"What?"

"Tony Stewart," she repeated.

"What's a Tony Stewart?" I asked.

"Tony Stewart!" She almost shouted.

I stood there open mouthed and confused.

"He is the NASCAR driver for Home Depot," she said with a touch of disbelief in her voice.

I looked at my brother-in-law who also had a look of disbelief on his face.

"I'm sorry," I said. "I know nothing about NASCAR."

"Take the Tony Stewart," brother-in-law said. "They'll like that."

I agreed and paid the clerk just in time to hear my brother-in-law mutter "Let's go look at French doors."

Out of the corner of my eye I saw shake him his head in disbelief as he gave a look of comfort to the clerk. In my innocence, I put the card in my pocket and followed him to the door section trying to look cool, while feeling that all eyes were on me and people were pointing and saying things like, "He's NASCAR challenged."

Native American Roots

I have been engaged in genealogical research so long that some folks accuse me of collecting dead relatives. I don't mind. Some of those I have collected were Cherokee.

They came out of the mountains of south western North Carolina and eventually wound up in Arkansas and Oklahoma. They made the journey before the Trail of Tears and were among those some called Old Settlers.

Our family tradition recognized this but we never talked about it much. In fact, I said that to a Ute woman working at the Southern Ute Museum in Ignacio, Colorado, and she responded with a smile, "I have white blood and I don't talk about it much either." Touché.

I have always felt an affinity for Native Americans and in my lifetime, I have had the great joy of knowing many. Among them Osage, Cherokee, Creek, Choctaw, Chickasaw, Apache, Lakota, and Dine (white folks call them Navajo). Joe Prater, my good friend's mother was Choctaw. An Iroquois friend gave me a medicine rattle on my 25th anniversary as a pastor. I have round danced with Ute and White Mountain Apache at celebrations I have attended. All of this to say I enjoy attending Native American events and feel a kinship with Native Americans.

So, this past July Miss Susan and I had the pleasure of visiting the Arapaho and Shoshone Indian Encampment at Cheyenne Frontier Days and in October we attended the Fourth Annual Octoraro Native American Fall Festival at Camp John Ware north of Conowingo, Maryland. It was a gorgeous fall day. I ate buffalo steak and danced there, as well.

Native American religion and tradition are among my favorite historical subjects. Therefore, I have a lot of books in my library covering those fields. I am especially struck by the native understanding of our connection with the earth and all living creatures. All of us could learn a lot by exploring a faith-based religion that refuses to separate the human animal from all that exists in nature.

Of course, one of the sad things about learning this history is how those of European heritage have desecrated everything Native Americans held and hold dear: land, water, trees, all plants and animals. And those of us called mixed bloods are constantly at war within ourselves as we struggle with those diverging attitudes.

That's enough of the old soapbox. Until later, ride on.

Now I Get It!

I was riding a trail the other day when I had an epiphany. After all these years, I finally got it!

If you drive into a restaurant and order a hot cup coffee and place it between your legs and drive away and it spills on you and your crotch is scalded you blame the restaurant.

If a teenager kills himself, you blame rock and roll music or the musician he liked.

If you smoke three packs of cigarettes every day and get lung cancer, you sue the tobacco company.

If your daughter gets pregnant by the football captain, you blame the school and its sex education classes.

If a feller gets drunk and crashes into a tree while driving home you blame the bartender.

If your children or grandchildren are certified brats, you blame television.

If a deranged lunatic shoots folks on the street, you blame the gun manufacturer.

So, it's all clear to me now. All the bad stuff that happens to folks is someone else's fault.

So, if I die while my wrinkled old behind is parked in front of this computer blame Bill Gates.

Oddity

Miss Susan and I were on a research trip for a novel I was writing about young men serving in the Cherokee Mounted Rifles during the Civil War. So, we traveled through the Cherokee Nation in eastern Oklahoma where most of the action takes place. During the trip, we visited the Cherokee National Historical Museum, of which I am a member, and while there took a tour of a replica of a Cherokee village before Europeans "discovered" them.

The young woman leading our tour was very knowledgeable and obviously had been doing this for some time. She showed us the council house, long house, winter and summerhouses and explained how they were built of reeds and clay. She also explained their uses.

She explained the pottery making method of ancient Cherokees. We have used it in elementary school where they have you roll out long strings of clay and then coil them up one of top of another to make a pot. The difference is they fired their pots in a campfire by burying it deep in the hot coals overnight.

Along the way, she told of how the ancient Cherokee used blowguns to kill small prey for food. Then, took a river reed and demonstrated how they hollowed it out to make a blowgun. The darts were made of slim whittled and shaped sticks and feathered with the fluffy white stuff found inside thistle pods. I shared with her that I had a bunch of it in my pasture for a couple of years and tried to kill it off. I never knew it had any purpose.

That done, she took a blowgun slipped a dart into it and with one puff sent the dart flying to its target. Turning to me, she smiled and said, "Would you like to try it, sir?"

Of course! Anyone silly enough to get on a bareback bronc will try anything once. I took the blowgun, loaded a dart, and blew. It sailed about three feet and fell to the ground. She laughed and said, "You need to take a deep breath before you blow, sir."

I did and I hit the target.

As we moved through the village, she shared that each "town" had a war chief and a peace chief, as well as a respected older woman called "The Beloved One." The Beloved One had as much power as the chiefs and could easily overrule them as they carried out the will of the People. The elders of the village, she told us, were held in high esteem.

"What would that make me," I asked. "I'm almost seventy."

Without dropping a beat she replied, "An oddity." Then quickly added, "Forty-five was the average lifespan in those days."

It was fascinating journey through another time. Miss Susan, however, keeps sharing with folks that she is married to an oddity. Oh, well, I can still ride on.

Out to Lunch

Some forty years as a writer, sometime newspaper editor, and teacher has made me a little critical of the way folks express themselves. When I was attending Pittsburg State University back in Kansas, one of our English professors published an annual collection of the worst essays he received for the year. He called it "Out to Lunch."

Well, I have collected some doozies myself. What follows is some analogies and metaphors found in essays by students from around the country all of whom will remain nameless.

"Her face was a perfect oval, like a circle that had its two other sides gently compressed by a Thigh Master."

"His thoughts tumbled in his head, making and breaking alliances like underpants in a dryer without Cling Free."

"Her hair glistened in the rain like nose hair after a sneeze."

"Her vocabulary was as bad as, like, whatever."

"He was as tall as a six-foot-three-inch tree."

"The hailstones leaped from the pavement, just like maggots when you fry them in hot grease."

"Long separated by cruel fate, star-crossed lovers raced across the grassy field toward each other like two freight trains, one having left Cleveland at 6:36 p.m. traveling at 55 mph, the other from Topeka at 4:19 p.m. at a speed of 35 mph."

"A politician was gone but unnoticed, like the period after the Dr. on a Dr Pepper can."

"John and Mary had never met. They were like two hummingbirds who had also never met."

"The thunder was ominous sounding, much like sound of a thin sheet of metal being shaken backstage during the storm scene in a play."

"The red brick wall was the color of a brick-red Crayola crayon."

He fell for her like his heart was a mob informant and she was the East River."

Even in his last years, Grandpappy had a mind like a steel trap, only one that had been left out so long, it had rusted shut."

"Shots rang out, as shots are wont to do."

"The plan was simple, like my brother-in-law Phil. But unlike Phil, this plan just might work."

"He was as lame as a duck. Not the metaphorical lame duck either, but a real duck that was actually lame. Maybe from stepping on a land mine or something."

"She had a deep, throaty, genuine laugh, like that sound a dog makes just before it throws up."

"It came down the stairs looking very much like something no one had ever seen before."

"The ballerina rose gracefully *en pointe* and extended one slender leg behind her, like a dog at a fire hydrant."

'The dandelion swayed in the gentle breeze like an oscillating electric fan set on medium."

"It was an American tradition, like fathers chasing kids around with power tools."

"He was deeply in love. When she spoke, he thought he heard bells, as if she were a garbage truck backing up."

"She grew on him like she was a colony of *E. coli* and he was room-temperature Canadian beef."

"She walked into my office like a centipede with 98 missing legs."

"It hurt the way your tongue hurts after you accidentally staple it to the wall."
And so forth. God help us and ride on.

Ownership and Responsibility

I have been thinking a lot about ownership these days. Not the ownership of my home, I do not own it. It belongs to Wells Fargo for the next two decades or until the fairy godmother of riches touches my old gray head. I am talking about the things all U.S. citizens own including radio and television airways.

I keep wondering why, if as a citizen I own the airways, there is little on radio or television that appeals to me. Oh, there is the history channel, Discovery, and a few others, but most of the time, the air is filled with ridiculous adolescent mind-mush or screaming ninnies who in their rude arrogance and ignorance spew hatred and lies, that many Americans accept as fact.

I may be old and slow, but I am not stupid. I know when the black and tan hound is chasing a rabbit instead of a raccoon. My daddy taught me that. Therefore, why do we allow this to continue? It sure is not culture, or news. When is the last time you spotted honest reporting on television and radio? I know. It is not a fair question, so don't let those brain cells burn up while you try to remember.

My first profession was journalism. My first degree was in journalism. I worked in both the print and broadcast medium. They taught me back then that the facts were important.

I once exposed some criminal behavior in the police department of a Missouri city where I was assistant editor and reporter on a daily newspaper. The editor read the story and took it and me into the publisher's office. We sat quietly while he read the story. Then he looked me in the eye and asked, "Is your source trustworthy?"

I could not tell him the source was a police officer, so I just said, "Yes."

He thought for a moment and then asked," Can you verify all this information?"

I responded, "Yes."

He looked at the editor and he looked at me and said, "Print it."

The story appeared in the paper that evening and was broadcast on the radio the next day. It brought the house down. Hearings were held. Heads rolled. It was the truth and that is what real journalism is all about. Telling the truth.

Accepting handouts from political and corporate figures and reporting them as fact is not good journalism.

Journalism insists that reporters to tell the truth. We have little of that on television and radio anymore. Most "news" is regurgitated pap handed top reporters by the powers and principalities with little basis in fact. It is designed to control and manipulate the masses. And, damn it, I am one of the masses and I am tired of it. How about you?

Promises, Promises

I don't usually like jokes about people dying, but this one is too good to keep to myself. It seems that when Abu al-Zarqawi was killed, he went to heaven and the first person he met at the Pearly Gates was George Washington who slapped him across the face and yelled, "How dare you try to destroy the nation I helped conceive?"

Then, Patrick Henry materialized and punched him in the nose and shouted, "You wanted to end our liberties but you failed!"

Jimmy Madison was next. He kicked him in the groin and said, "This is why I allowed our government to provide for the common defense!"

Tom Jefferson arrived and began beating al-Zarqawi about the head and shoulders with a long cane snarling, "It was evil men like you who inspired me to write the Declaration of Independence."

The beatings and thrashings continued as George Mason, James Monroe and a long line of other early Americans unleashed their anger on the terrorist leader.

As al-Zarqawi lay bleeding and in terrible pain, when the Prophet Mohammad appeared. Al-Zarqawi fell at his feet and began weeping.

"This is not what you promised me!" he cried.

Mohammad replied, "My son, it is exactly what I promised. I clearly said that for those who murder innocents in the name of Allah, there would be seventy-two Virginians waiting for them in the after-life. What did you think I said?"

Whoops!

Random Thoughts of a Retiree

I had amnesia once—or was it twice.

I went to San Francisco. I found someone's heart. Now what?

Protons have mass? I did not even know they were Catholic.

All I ask is a chance to prove that money cannot make me happy.

If the world were a logical place, men would be the ones to ride horses side-saddle.

What is a "free" gift? Aren't all gifts free?

They told me I was gullible … and I believed them.

Teach a child to be polite and courteous in the home and, when he grows up, he'll never be able to merge his car on I-95.

Two can live as cheaply as one, for half as long.

Experience is the thing you have left when everything else is gone.

What if there were no hypothetical questions?

One nice thing about egotists: They don't talk about other people.

When the only tool you own is a hammer, every problem begins to look like a nail.

A flashlight is a case for holding dead batteries.

Why do people say "close proximity"? Is there a "far proximity?"

My weight is perfect for my height—which varies.

I used to be indecisive. Now I'm not sure.

The cost of living hasn't affected its popularity.

What was the greatest thing before sliced bread?

How can there be self-help "groups"?

Is there another word for synonym?

What's another word for thesaurus?

What rhymes with orange?

Where do forest rangers go to "get away from it all"?

The speed of time is one-second per second.

Is it possible to be totally partial?

Is Marx's tomb a communist plot?

Show me a man with both feet firmly on the ground, and I'll show you a man who can't get his pants off.

Is it my imagination, or do buffalo wings taste like chicken?

They asked me if I had a problem being ignorant and apathetic. I told them, "I don't know and I don't care!"

Life is like a roll of toilet paper ... the closer you get to the end, the faster it goes.

Finally, Let me share two signs of senility: First is forgetfulness and I can't remember the other one.

If you've already heard accept my apology, check your cinch and ride on.

Remembering Margaret

My sister Margaret married a third generation Colorado rancher over fifty years ago. Early in October 2004, she was getting ready to move a tractor on their place. She stood on the ground and turned the ignition to start it the tractor. It lurched forward and crushed her to death. It was a shock, to say the least.

As we mourned her passing, I remembered all those little things we tend to remember about loved ones: the good and the bad. All four of my sisters are younger than I am. She was the two years younger and I treated her pretty badly when we were kids.

Once while she and Joy, the sister just younger then her, were riding double and bareback, I loped alongside them waved my cowboy hat and whooped. The horse they were riding made a sharp left turn. The two sisters did not. They landed in a patch of prickly pear with Margaret on the bottom and Joy on top. Mama had a long, tedious job pulling out all those cactus spines. And I suffered one in a long line of verbal punishments from Mama.

It should not have come as surprise. I teased and argued with Margaret from the moment she joined the family and displaced me as the only child. I know now that such rivalry is normal. As the oldest child in the family and the only son, as well as the oldest grandson in the family, I was aware of my intrinsic value. That is not to say I was spoiled. That is a discussion better left for another time.

When we were younger than the horse incident, an argument in the garden ended when I struck her lightly on the head with a hoe. In our advanced years, she still got a kick out of parting her thick silver hair to show folks the tiny scar. Another time, she insisted on me giving her a piggyback ride. I was in my imaginary horse mode and bucked her off. She hit the corner of a porch step with her chest. She also used that scar in our old age to embarrass me in front of guests, when I would visit her in Colorado. What a memory, she had. Nevertheless, she loved me and I loved her. She would embarrass me by bragging about me to her friends and I am not easy to embarrass.

So, this is a final word to Margaret. Hang in there girl. I pray your new adventure is a good one. And ride on.

Riding the Rattlesnake

Computers and their ilk are not always right. Miss Susan and I were headed to Spokane, Washington, this spring. Before leaving, I ask one of the computer travel sources how far it was from Spokane to Joseph, Oregon. With a smirk, the web site said, "Four hours, you big dummy. Why don't you look at a map?"

I looked at my AAA map. The distance shown in the road map seemed to fit the web site's snotty calculation. So, when our Frontier Airlines flight dropped us down onto the tarmac at Spokane we picked up a rental car and headed south for Nez Perce country. We had been traveling some twelve hours by then but another four hours would be easy to make on a pleasant drive through eastern Washington and Oregon. That was before we encountered the Rattlesnake.

We began by climbing up the side of a canyon and began a series of switch-backs to the bottom of the canyon. That's it, we said. That was interesting. Then the road took a little twist and started up the side of another canyon. We drove along looking out over the vast wilderness below us as we climbed high and higher. That must be it, we said, a little challenging but interesting. Then the road started down into another series of switchbacks toward the bottom of another canyon. We looked at each other exclaiming, "My sweet Lord! Is this ever going to end?" It didn't.

Soon we were going up another series of switchbacks. We could look up from the bottom of a canyon and see the roads twisting and turning their way above us. To make a long story a lot shorter this went on for what seemed like an eternity. We were supposed to reach our destination at 6 p.m. We arrived at nine just as darkness was cloaking the Wallowa Valley.

Our hostess met us and showed us to our quarters. She was kind and accommodating. When we apologized for our tardiness and began explaining why we were so late and so fatigued, she chuckled and said, "Oh, you came by way of Rattlesnake Grade."

We knew how it got its name. We were also unsure about taking the same route out of the valley. Is there any other way back to Spokane, we asked. Of course, she said. However, it is three hours longer. Other residents told us they drive it every week to go to Costco and other stores and laughed as they said we should have driven it in the old days when it was a narrow little roadway without appropriate guardrails. We were thankful about the improvements and after resting for a few days we rode the Rattlesnake back toward Spokane. It is better when you are rested and in no hurry. In fact, it is a beautiful drive.

Signs That You Have Grown Up

I refuse to grow up! If it means ridding yourself of a mind filled with adventuresome thoughts, then I am not interested. From time to time one of my daughters will suggest that growing up might be good for a man of my age. Nope. Not interested.

To make matters worse Texas cousin Charlie sent me as list of things that prove one is grown up. I don't know that I agree with them all but some of them may make sense to those of you who want to be grown up.

1. Your houseplants are alive, and you cannot smoke any of them.

2. Making love in a single bed is out of the question.

3. You keep more food than beer in the icebox.

4. 6:00 a.m. is when you get up, not when you go to bed.

5. You hear your favorite song in an elevator.

6. You find yourself watching the Weather Channel.

7. Your friends marry and divorce instead of "hook up" and break up."

8. You go from 130 days of holidays to 20.

9. Jeans and a sweater no longer qualify as "dressed up." Sorry, Charlie, for me a starched white shirt and starched creased jeans with clean boots is still dressed up.

10. You are the one calling the police because the kids next door will not turn down the stereo.

11. Older relatives feel comfortable telling sex jokes around you.

12. Your car insurance goes down and your car payments go up.

13. You feed your dog Science Diet instead of McDonald's leftovers.

14. Sleeping on the couch makes your back hurt.

15. You take naps from noon to 6 pm. Mine are two to five, so I am still not growing up.

16. Dinner and a movie is the whole date instead of the beginning of one. For some of us, dinner and movie is eating at home and watching a DVD.

17. Eating a basket of barbecued chicken wings at 3 am would severely upset, rather than settle, your stomach. That's true no matter how old you are ... and by the way how did they ever come with a name like "buffalo wings."

18. A $4.00 bottle of wine is no longer "pretty good stuff."

19. You actually eat breakfast food at breakfast time.

20. "I just can't drink the way I used to" replaces "I'm never going to drink that much again."

21. 90% of the time you spend in front of a computer is for real work. Alright, you got me there.

22. You read this entire list looking desperately for one sign that doesn't apply to you and can't find one.

Silly Churches

Early in my career as a preacher I served rural churches in Kansas, Missouri and Maryland. But, they were nothing like the hillbilly churches that Blind Tom Harper, my alter ego fictional pastor friend, served. We're both retired, so we have a lot of time to visit and he told me a fascinating story the other day.

He said he served a church where the finance committee refused to provide funds for the purchase of a chandelier because none of the members knew how to play one.

I thought that was silly until he told me that one Sunday some of the folks asked him whether the two fish Jesus used to feed the 5000 were bass or catfish, and what bait did he use to catch 'em.

Now, I've held church services in a snowstorm where only me and the widow next door to church were in attendance after she built the fire in the stove that heated the church and waited to see if I would make it. But, Tom bested me on many oddities about the church. For instance they use Boone's Farm "Tickle Pink" for communion and there were only seven last names in the church directory.

I've heard baptisms called "dunking" and "doing the baby" but he said folks in that church referred to baptism as "branding."

I told Tom served churches where you had to hold it or use an old outhouse. But, Blind Tom wouldn't be dissuaded. He said, finding and returning lost sheep isn't just a parable in that parish and his folks think rapture is what you get when you lift something too heavy and they use a #2 galvanized washtub for baptismal font."

I said, "Now you're making things up."

He said, "Nope. Their choir robes were donated by (and embroidered with the logo from) Billy Bob's Barbecue and the collection plates were hub caps from a '56 Chevy."

I gave up.

Social Security

Old Beans came wandering in the other day, poured himself a cup of coffee and sat down at the kitchen table. He didn't say much, so we just sipped our coffee, looked at the kitchen window, and watched the horses graze. Finally, I asked him what was bothering him. That's always a mistake, because he'll tell you.

"I been reading," he said.

I took a deep breath. Anytime Beans reads, it can be traumatic. He looked me in the eye and saw the fear, grinned a little and then let loose.

"With all the hoopla about Social Security," he said, "I decided to do some research instead of believing whatever comes out of the boob-tube. Did you know that before the first Social Security check was mailed in 1937, Alf Landon was predicting it was a failure during his campaign stops when he was running against FDR?"

I had to admit I didn't know that.

"Then," he said, "in 1964, Senator Barry Goldwater, declared the system was collapsing. Then, Ronald Reagan came along in the 1980's calling for privatization. Now, we have Dubya saying the same thing."

"Nothing new, then," I said.

"Right."

He sipped his coffee before continuing.

"All of these folks say just want to "save" the program. But, you know I found out all the Wall Street are licking the chops. They're like a bunch of buzzards circling road kill."

"Is that right?" I asked.

"Durn tootin'," he said as he sipped his coffee. "And all these groups that are for fixin' Social Security by cutting out part of it for private investment are all in cahoots. Just look at them: the National Association of Manufacturers, Securities Industry Association, the U.S. Chamber of Commerce, Paine Webber, Charles Schwab, Wachovia Bank, Cato Institute, all the big boys in investment. They are quietly ganging up on old folks and those who will be old someday."

"Sounds scarey."

"It is," he said. "But, there's something even scarier."

"What's that?"

"These old boys don't know their eye from their elbow."

"You been reading something else?"

"You got it, hoss," he said. "First, they keep saying the fund will be bankrupt by 2042. Ain't true. Even if it continues as is, the fund can pay 80% of Social Security for a long time after 2042. And, on top of that, old Dubya wants to borrow $15 trillion dollars to convert the system to private accounts. That's a lot of debt."

"How many zeros in 15 trillion," I asked.

"Got me," Old Beans said. "I just know that's a lot of money."

"So, what do folks do?"

"Make 'em tell the truth."

Tardy

As I have said before I have a real problem with being late for anything. Some say it is a psychological problem and not a good one. Some claim it is compulsive behavior needing serious treatment. Others just say I'm weird. In fact, one of many nicknames I picked up as a young man was "Old Weird Vern." But, never call me that to my face. It upsets me and that is another issue with which I have never dealt. Whatever, the case, I hate being late for anything and I have little sympathy for anyone's excuse, which brings to mind an old story.

It seems a preacher was being honored at his retirement dinner after 25 years of ministry. A leading local politician and member of the congregation was chosen to make the presentation and give a little speech at the dinner. He was delayed, so the preacher decided to say his own few words while they waited.

"I got my first impression of the parish from the first confession I heard here," he said. "I thought I had been assigned to a terrible place when the very first person who came to me confessed me he had stolen a television set; and, when questioned by the police, was able to lie his way out of it. He had stolen money from his parents, embezzled from his employer, had an affair with his boss's wife; taken illegal drugs, and gave venereal disease to his sister. I was appalled. But as the days went on I knew that you people were not all like that and I had, indeed, come to a fine parish full of good and loving people."

Just as the preacher finished his talk, the politician arrived full of apologies at being late and he immediately began to make the presentation and gave his scheduled talk.

"I'll never forget the first day our preacher arrived," said the politician. "In fact, I had the honor of being the first one to go to him in confession."

The moral is very clear: DON'T EVER BE LATE!

Tater and the Trout

My old friend, some say my alter ego, Tater Johnson was stopped by a game warden recently leaving a spot well known for its trout fishing in Colorado. He had a long string of rainbows and was feeling pretty good about the day.

The game warden asked Tater, "Do you have a license to catch all those fish?"

"Naw," Tater said. "I ain't got no license. These here are my pet fish."

"Pet fish?" the game warden asked. "I have never heard of anyone having rainbow trout for pets."

"Well," Tater said. "I do. Every night I take these fish down to the river and let 'em swim 'round for a while. Then I whistle and they jump right back into this ice chest and I take 'em home."

"That's a bunch of bull!" the game warden said as he reached for his citation book. "Trout can't do that! In fact, no fish can do that!"

Tater looked at the game warden for a moment and then said, "It's the truth. I'll show you. It really works."

"Okay," the game warden said. Show me. I've got to see this!"

Tater poured the fish back into the lake and stood and waited.

After several minutes, the game warden turned to him and said, "Well?"

"Well, what?" said Tater.

"When are you going to call them back?"

"Call who back?"

"The FISH!"

Tater scratched his head and said, "What fish?"

The Agony of Looking Back

Having passed my seventy-third birthday, I realized I have seen some amazing things. An old acquaintance my age said, "You know, we probably witnessed more than anyone in our time." He was talking about all that happened in the fifties, sixties, seventies, eighties, etc. And he was right. Then, I ran on to some statistics from 1905 when my daddy was only four years old.

- The average life expectancy in the U.S. was 47 years.

- Only 14 percent of the homes in the U.S. had a bathtub.

- Only 8 percent of the homes had a telephone. Lucky devils.

- A three-minute call from Denver to New York City cost eleven dollars.

- There were only 8,000 cars in the U.S., and only 144 miles of paved roads and no one was talking on a telephone while trying to run you down, which would have been hard since the maximum speed limit in most cities was 10 mph.

- Alabama, Mississippi, Iowa, and Tennessee were each more heavily populated than California which only had 1.4 million people and was the 21st most populous state in the Union.

- The tallest structure in the world was the Eiffel Tower!

- The average wage in the U.S. was 22 cents per hour and the average worker made between $200 and $400 per year.

- A competent accountant could expect to earn $2000 per year. It didn't say how much an incompetent accountant earned.

- A dentist earned $2,500 per year. Now-a-days that one root canal.

- A veterinarian earned between $1,500 and $4,000 per year. We pay that much ourselves for our three horses.

- More than 95 percent of all births in the U.S. took place at home.

- Ninety percent of all U.S. doctors had no college education. Instead, they attended so-called medical schools, many of which were condemned in the press and by the government as "substandard."

- Sugar cost four cents a pound, eggs were fourteen cents a dozen and coffee was fifteen cents a pound.

- Most women only washed their hair once a month, and used borax or egg yolks for shampoo.

- Canada passed a law that prohibited poor people from entering into their country for any reason.

- The leading causes of death in the U.S. were pneumonia, influenza, tuberculosis, diarrhea, heart disease, and stroke.

- The flag of the United States had 45 stars, since Arizona, Oklahoma, New Mexico, Hawaii, and Alaska had not been admitted to the Union.

- The population of Las Vegas, Nevada, was 30!

- Crossword puzzles, canned beer, and ice tea hadn't been invented yet.

- There was no Mother's Day or Father's Day.

- Two out of every ten U.S. adults couldn't read or write.

- Only 6 percent of all Americans had graduated from high school.

- Marijuana, heroin, and morphine were all available over the counter at the local corner drugstores and your local pharmacist said, "Heroin clears the complexion, gives buoyancy to the mind, regulates the stomach and bowels, and is, in fact, a perfect guardian of health."

- Eighteen percent of households in the U.S. had at least one full-time servant or domestic help.

- There were about 230 reported murders in the entire U.S.

Ride on!

The Coldsmith Special

I met Don Coldsmith at a convention in Nevada and discovered we have a lot in common. Like me, he writes a column filled with odds and ends. His column is called "Horsin' Around." Like me, he is a Methodist. He is the son of a Kansas Methodist preacher. He did his basic training in World War II with a mule based mountain artillery unit. The recruiter who lied me into the army said I would be assigned to that unit during the Korean War. The reality was that the unit was disbanded before I finished basic training. That's another story.

Unlike me, Don has written some thirty books, primarily the Spanish Bit series and books about the tall grass prairie of the Kansas Flint Hills. I've read them all and I recommend them to you. But, that's not the point of the story, either.

The point is when he retired after thirty years as a family practice physician he found himself home writing, ranching, and waiting for his wife to come home after a hard day's work. That's kind of like me, as well. In the process of trying to be a thoughtful husband, he began cooking the evening meal. He came up with a nifty recipe. I use it. I call the Coldsmith special.

Here it is. Get out the trusty crock-pot. Slice an onion in the bottom; put a steak on top of the onions. Mix one third cup of brown sugar, one third cup of salsa, one third cup of catsup. Pour that over the steak and turn the sucker on to slow cook all day. If that's not enough chow for your big family just another layer like the first.

When it's done you can serve it with any side dishes you want. I just eat the meat and onions and enjoy myself. Give it a shot, check your cinch now and then and ride on.

The Conversion of Tater Johnson

My boyhood friend Tater Johnson converted. He was the descendent of a long line of Ozark Mountain Baptists but he has converted to Catholicism. This is how I heard the story from one of his relatives.

Every Friday night after work, Tater would fire up his grill in the back yard of his little house by the Katy railroad tracks. He would throw a big Angus steak on it along with a bunch of potatoes wrapped in aluminum foil and stand there smelling the aroma and sipping a cold beer. Now, Tater's neighbors were all Catholics and to make matters worse, they had all been instructed not to eat meat on Fridays during Lent. However, the smell of steak cooking was almost more than they could stand, so they asked their priest to come visit Tater.

He did. While they were chatting, he suggested Tater convert to Catholicism so he would be just like his neighbors. Tater was never too much of a theologian. In fact, he was a Baptist just because his momma and her people were Baptists. And he liked this young Irish priest. So, he took the required classes and attended Mass. And then one day, he took the plunge, so to speak.

In front of his neighbors and to the consternation of his family and in violation of all theological premises, he was rebaptized. The priest sprinkled holy water on him and declared

"You were born a Baptist and raised a Baptist, but now you are Catholic."

Well, to put it mildly Tater's neighbors were ecstatic and greatly relieved that no longer would they be tempted by Tater's cookouts. Then, Friday night arrived and the wonderful aroma of grilled Angus steak filled the neighborhood.

Frantic, they called the priest and he rushed to Tater's house clutching a rosary and a prayer book, prepared to scold this backslider. He was about to speak out against Tater's proclivity to eat meat on Friday when he stopped in amazement and watched Tater lift a small bottle of water and carefully sprinkled the grilling meat chanting: "You wuz born an Angus, and you wuz raised an Angus, but now you are a catfish."

The Greatest Generation

Those of us who lived during World War II did not have to be told by Tom Brokaw that those who served were the "greatest generation."

With all their differences, and there were many, these people understood the world stood on the brink of fascist destruction. They came together, these kids, and they were just kids, and fought a terrible war. For many like Bill Owens, my father-in-law, it was the ultimate adventure and high-mark of achievement in their lives.

They had families, children, love and respect in their community and they carried within them strength that comes with the bonding of war, steel that comes from the fire of shared experiences. A solid sense of purpose with an honorable foundation and a clear-cut goal shaped those kids and turned them into men and women who knew whom they were and knew their role in community and nation.

My father-in-law, died in early November, 2003. I regret never telling him about my respect for him. . It seems the time is never right to express those things to people we love until they part the curtain and exit our lives. Difficult as it was, I tried to do that in his eulogy.

Bill set an example. He spent twenty five years as a basketball referee, thirty one years as football referee and perhaps, most importantly thirty three years coaching and shaping young men of every age on baseball teams in southeast Kansas. He provided leadership for the Telephone Pioneers, Veterans of Foreign Wars and the American Legion. Not a unique man for his time, he did as so many others of that generation did: he gave back to the community that nurtured him.

It never seemed to me that he was especially fond of me, but when the grandchildren came along the distance began to shrink. Still, we were never buddy-buddy. Then, a few years after my mother-in-law Glennice passed, I was returning from teaching one summer in Colorado and stopped by to say hello. We visited a little and finally, I got up to go. He stood and I extended my hand for a farewell handshake. He grabbed me and hugged me.

Now, not much ever surprises me and I am not often taken off guard, but he had me cold. I went out to my old pick-em-up truck and called Miss Susan. She thought it was funny when I exclaimed, "Your dad hugged me!"

I suspect he got a kick out of my surprise, because he had a deep mischievous streak in him. Nevertheless, what he had mostly was a powerful love of family and country. Like most men of his generation, he did not show it in a physical or emotional way. However, as he got older, he found comfort in his children and delight in his grandchildren and great-grandchildren. The true love of life remained Glennice. In these last years, he really missed her and was frustrated by the fact that she beat him to the other side.

We mourned his passing knowing that we mourned for ourselves and we celebrated his life: a life filled with duty, strength, and most of all—love. We miss him.

Thinking Again

I was talking with some cousins back in my hometown and we reminisced about the old days. Several of them have followed their fathers' footsteps and are in the car business. Someone in the group mentioned fender skirts. Now, that, I thought is one of those terms that have disappeared from our language with hardly a notice. It has company. Curb feelers and steering knobs are also outdated in the world of automobiles. Any youngsters reading this column may have to find someone over fifty to explain things to them.

Remember "Continental kits?" They were rear bumper extenders and spare tire covers that were supposed to make any car as cool as a Lincoln Continental. They didn't but that was their advertised purpose.

Then there was a thing called emergency brakes. At some point, parking brake took its place. But, there was a hint of drama when you called it an emergency brake. And the foot feed became the accelerator. Remember, how exciting it was to ride on the running board of the car while your dad idled up the driveway.

A phrase heard all the time in my youth on a Kansas farm and never hear anymore is "store-bought." Of course, just about everything is store-bought these days. However, once it gave you bragging rights to have a store-bought dress or shirt that was not made at home from flowered feed sacks. And a store-bought bag of candy was a real treat.

"Coast to coast" was a phrase that once held all sorts of excitement and now it means almost nothing. We even take the term "worldwide" for granted.

On a smaller scale, "wall-to-wall" was once a magical term in our homes. In the '50s, everyone moved from covering their hardwood floors with linoleum to wall-to-wall carpeting! Today, everyone replaces their wall-to-wall carpeting with hardwood floors. That's just downright confusing.

How about the term "in a family way?" It's hard to imagine that the word "pregnant" was once considered a little too graphic, a little too clinical for use in polite company. But, it was and we that talked about stork visits and "being in a family way" or simply "expecting."

It's hard to recall that this word "divorce" was once said in a whisper. And no one is called a "divorcee" anymore. Certainly not a "gay divorcee." Come to think of it, "confirmed bachelors" and "career girls" are long gone, too.

We used to go to town on Saturdays to shop and take in a "picture show." We all thought calling it a "movie" or a "motion picture" was an affectation.

Most of these words go back to the '50s or earlier, but here's a pure-'60s word I heard the other day: "rat fink." Now, that places the speaker in a different time warp. And how about "percolator." That was just a neat word. It has been replaced by "Coffeemaker." How dull! It's all Mr. Coffee's fault.

I also miss made-up marketing words that were meant to sound so modern and now sound so retro. Words like "DynaFlow" and "Electrolux." Introducing the 1963 Admiral TV, now with "SpectraVision!"

And by the way, when did they wipe out that unique health hazard called lumbago? No one complains of that anymore. Maybe that's what castor oil cured, because I never hear mothers threatening their kids with castor oil anymore.

Some words aren't gone, but are definitely on the endangered list. When I was a boy, dinner was the noon meal and supper was the evening meal. Lunch is what you carried in a bucket to school or work.

It is time to act.

- Save the language.

- Invite someone to supper.

- Discuss fender skirts.

- Refuse to become modernized.

Hope is born, when we are willing to die for the right things, so check your cinch and ride on.

True Intellectual Challenges

Out in my old home state of Kansas, a newcomer moved into a rural area. After living there a while he called the local township administrative office and requested the removal of the Deer Crossing sign on a road near his house. The reason: "Too many deer were being hit by cars." He did not want them to cross there anymore.

This should surprise no one. A woman went to a local Taco Bell and ordered a taco. She asked the person behind the counter for "minimal lettuce." The counter person responded, "Sorry, we only have iceberg lettuce."

At an airport check in gate in Birmingham, Alabama, the security person asked, "Has anyone put anything in your baggage without your knowledge? The passenger to be replied, "If it was without my knowledge, how would I know?" The security officer smiled knowingly and nodded, "That's why we ask."

Out in Wichita, Kansas, they have stoplights on the corners that buzz when it is safe to cross the street. One intellectually challenged person asked a coworker if they knew what the buzzer was for. When her friend said no, she explained that it signals blind people when the light is red. Appalled, the intellectual challenged woman responded, "What on earth are blind people doing driving?"

At a good-bye luncheon for an old and dear coworker who was leaving the company due to "downsizing," a manager commented cheerfully, "this is fun. We should do this more often." Not a word was spoken. The folks at Texas Instruments just looked at each other with that deer in the headlights stare.

One man worked with an individual who plugged her power strip back into itself and for the life of her could not understand why her computer system would not turn on. She was a deputy with the Dallas County Sheriff's office, no less.

When a couple arrived at an automobile dealership to pick up their car, they were told the keys had been locked in it. They went to the service department and found a mechanic working feverishly to unlock the driver's side door. As they watched from the passenger side, the wife instinctively tried the door handle and discovered that it was unlocked. "Hey," she announced to the technician, "its open!" To which he replied, "I know—I already got that side." This is a true story and it happened at the Ford dealership in Canton, Mississippi!

A word of caution: They walk among us ... *and* REPRODUCE!

So, ride on—carefully.

Tying Vine Deloria's Tie

At a meeting of western historians and writers, I had the privilege of meeting the late Lakota Indian writer Vine Deloria, Jr. Some of you may remember his seminal book "Custer Died for Your Sins." He wrote much more but that is the one that placed him in the forefront of western writers and historians.

As we gathered for an evening banquet, Vine entered the room with his wife Shirley. Suffering from back trouble, he used a cane and sat as often as possible. Since I always sit near the back of these kinds of events, I was sitting at a table near the entrance with a historian from Canada. I sit in those places just in case I get bored. That way I can slip away. Vine limped to my table and sat heavily in a chair near me. He reached into his suit jacket pocket and pulled forth an old, short wrinkled tie. As he threaded it under his shirt collar and began trying to tie it, it was obvious he didn't wear a tie very often. He struggled a bit and then his wife tried it. It still wasn't tied properly. It was upside down and crooked. He said, "I used to tie a tie running from the barracks for roll call in the army."

I saw my chance.

I said, "Me, too. Would you like me to tie it?"

He said, "Go ahead."

I stood and walked around him, reached around to straighten his tie and then asked, "Would a half-Windsor do?"

The old Indian said, "Any way you want to tie it is fine."

So, I tied Vine Deloria's tie.

He thanked me and the Deloria's proceeded to the head table. The Canadian woman next to me said, "You just tied Vine Deloria's tie."

"Bragging rights," I said.

"And I saw you do it"" she replied.

"That may be important if I brag about it and someone thinks I'm not telling truth."

"I understand," she said. "If you need confirmation, I'm your witness."

Well, I can tell the story, but I've forgotten her name. If you want to verify the story go to British Columbia and go to every college and university and ask for the woman who witnessed an old white haired guy tie Vine Deloria's tie.

Wedding Bells, Wagon Ruts
and
Wyoming

One year in early September, I had the honor of officiating at the wedding of Miss Susan's nephew in Cheyenne, Wyoming. Everything went pretty much as planned. He and his beautiful bride got off to a good start. They hit it big with the gifts and then headed to Cancun for their honeymoon after I reminded them that Cancun and those other tourist traps were not the real Mexico. I try to throw cold water on every good moment that occurs.

The only thing curious about the event was at the wedding place, the little historic army chapel on the F.E. Warren Air Base. There were a lot of armed men in the congregation. Both the bride and the groom are police officers and half the congregation was made up of cops. I joked about rather than a shotgun wedding we had a Biretta wedding.

Following a night of revelry in which Miss Susan and I nearly danced our legs off, we rested up for a day or so and then headed north for a little tourist time. One of the stops was the ruts of the Oregon Trail.

In the mid-seventies, Miss Susan, I, and our girls lived near the old trail in Kansas. It started in what is now the Kansas City, Missouri, area and wound across eastern Kansas where it went north along the Blue River until it reached the Platte River in Nebraska. It then followed the Platte west, a river one wag called "an inch deep and a mile wide." The California Trail and the Mormon Trail both followed basically the same route until reaching a point in western Wyoming where they divided to go their separate ways.

A lot of newly weds, like our nephew and new niece, took the trips, as well as whole families and some single folk. What is recorded history but seldom mentioned is that thousands of them are buried along the trail. I thought about that as we stood along the winding Platte looking at ruts worn deep in the earth. Perhaps, the most fascinating aspect of the site were the four to six feet deep ruts worn in sandstone hills marking where the wagons found their way over them.

Miss Susan stood shoulder deep in the ruts declaring the impossibility of wagons having made the ruts. Once convinced that the iron rims of thousands of wagons passing through the area had indeed made the deep ruts, she joined her sister, brother-in-law and me walking some of the trail. At one point I wandered off alone and stood on a hill overlooking a level area near the river where Captain John C. Fremont, his guide, Kit Carson, and cartographer Carl Pruess camped with their troops in the early nineteenth century. Gazed out over the rolling hills and waving grass, I wondered why anyone would have traveled any farther. I would have just pitched my tent right there and stayed. Looking out over the rolling hills covered with waving grass, I even thought I saw a herd of buffalo and I was riding my old mare to get closer for the hunt in the early afternoon sunshine. But, no! It was just my imagination. Ahhh ...

2.

Another July, I joined Miss Susan, her sister, Barbara, and Barbara's husband, Ernest in Cheyenne, Wyoming, for the Cheyenne Frontier Days.

Miss Susan had been there twice before, but I never made it until this year. I guess the in-laws got tired of my whining "When I die I want my tombstone to read, "He never got to see the Daddy of 'Em All."

The "Daddy of 'Em All" is what they call ten days of bronc riding, calf and steer roping, bull riding, steer wrestling, barrel racing, pancake breakfasts, Indian encampments, parades, and other hoopla.

Cheyenne, along with several other western towns, claim to have the first organized rodeo in the country. It's a toss-up between some of them, but it's a fun way to exercise bragging rights.

Rodeo began when cowboys from different ranches would compete against one another after roundup. In those days it was primarily saddle bronc riding, steer wrestling and roping.

Bill Picket, a black Texas cowboy, is sort of the daddy of steer wrestling. They used to call it bulldogging. Picket had seen a bulldog bring a steer down by grabbing its nose and lips with its teeth. He bet he could do it. And did. Hence the term "bulldogging."

Saddle bronc riding was not an eight-second exercise like it is today. The old cowboys rode bucking horses almost daily. The competition was to see who could stay until the baddest of the bad horses quit bucking.

Roping? Well, ropers still exist. Oklahoma cowboy Will Rogers made trick roping famous in his vaudeville comedy act by billing himself as "The Ropin' Fool." Ropers are a different breed. They start young and will rope anything that exists. I've seen them rope barn cats and dogs, grandmas and cousins. I'm not a died in the wool roper, bu5t I've even roped noisy nephews and an occasional horseback rider. Why? 'Cause I felt the urge. Ropers will even rope stuff that isn't alive. Fence posts, little plastic steer heads stuck in a bale of hay, their own boots while sitting down. Odd fellows, those ropers.

Anyhow, I got to see some of the best at Cheyenne. If you ever get the chance, take it,

3.

One year in Wyoming we visited old Ft. Laramie. My primary reason for the visit was my interest in the history of the old west. However, I had been encouraged to visit the place by Mike Moore, an expert in the fur trade and the mountain men of yore and a writer friend.

Ft. Laramie was established as a fur trading post in 1834 by William Sublette and others. It sat on a point above a river that had been name Laramie by some French trappers prior to Sublette's arrival. It seems one of the trappers named Jacques La Ramie was found looking like a pincushion for Indian arrows. I guess they named the place as a memorial. Anyway it stuck.

Ft. William, as it was called for a time before that. It was palisaded. That is, logs were stuck upright in the ground with pointed tops to surround the fort. I have oftened wondered about the tradition of doing that. Arlo Guthrie once noted that it was silly to do that since Indian knew about sharp points and gates. His theory was the pioneers did that to protect themselves from giant clams. But, that's another story.

Ft. William was a major fur trading and strategic business center after Sublette sold out to the American Fur Company. They held a fur trade monopoly until 1841 when Ft. Platte was built a mile away by another company. When this happened, they upgraded it, replacing the old wooden structure with adobe buildings and renaming it Ft. John. However, it usually went by the name of Ft. Laramie. It was a stopping place for pioneers on the Oregon Trail and by 1849; the usually peaceful Indians were becoming more and more uncomfortable with the influx of whites. Therefore, the army bought the place and turned it into a military post.

It eventually began to deteriorate and the army laid out a new post around a large parade ground, seldom used. They built stables, a bakery, officer and enlisted men's quarters. Troops varied at the post. Mounted riflemen and infantry were originally posted there, although it remains a mystery why the army, in its wisdom, sent infantry to combat some of the best light cavalry in the world.

On our tour, we learned that most of the soldiers stationed there never saw a hostile Indian. They did what the army always does: drill, parade, police the area, clean barracks, and kill time. Now and then, they took a trip to the nearby "hog ranches" where they drank a little and spent their pitiful salaries on the women.

Interesting to me was the fact that many of the frontier troops were recent immigrant Germans, Irish and others from Eastern Europe. Few spoke English, or really understood it. Desertion rate on the frontier on the frontier was 33% between 1865 and 1890. Seems like they would just get tired and walk away. I thought about that during my own basic training at Ft. Riley, Kansas, but never had the courage to follow up. Besides, in those days you could just disappear in the west.

Overall, it was a great visit and even with slashed budgets, the National Park Service is valiantly struggling to do its job. One interesting piece of information I ran onto while visiting the place was the bakery. They had a huge oven where the bakers held forth. These guys had to bake 700 eighteen ounce loaves of bread each and every day to feed the troops. The recipe is simple. It can be found in a book printed by the General Printing Office of the United States. It is called "Practical Instructions in Bread Making." Since I like to do a recipe column, now and then, I thought I would share it with you, just in case you have a crowd coming for the holidays and need to whip up a lot of homemade bread to feed them.

Those old boys in dirty shirt blue that served at those frontier posts turned baking into a simple science. They started by laying out basic ingredients: Salt, water, flour, lard and powdered yeast. Now pay close attention.

1. Into a bowl, pour four cups of lukewarm water. Dissolve two table-spoons of yeast, then mix in four cups of unsifted flour. Let sponge (that's the stuff you just mixed) sit covered with a towel in a warm place for one hour.

2. Then, add five more cups lukewarm water, two tablespoons salt and seven to nine cups of flour until the doughy consistency is reached. Mix well, kneading in a bowl. Set aside in a warm place for one hour, covered.

3. Return (you will have to do that if you want to continue with the process) and knead on a flat lightly floured surface. Return dough to bowl, coat surface with lard and set aside for one hour.

4. Then, knead the dough lightly and cut into twenty-ounce loaves. Place into greased pans, coating loaves again lightly with lard. Cover and let rise.

5. When sufficiently raised, place the pans in an oven preheated to 400 degrees. Bake 30 to 45 minutes or until golden brown. Remove, coat freshly baked bread with lard.

6. This recipe will make approximately eight 18 ounce loaves.

I told Miss Susan I was going to try the recipe and she remarked on my mental state before saying, "Just make sure you cut the recipe into smaller amounts!"

Give it a shot and don't forget the lard! And if you are ever out that way, stop in and take a tour. It is worth the time and effort.

Why I Love Children

Before I became a bootleg preacher, I was a regular pastor and I had the pleasure to meet many children. They were so interesting I began collecting stories about children. They are so wise and uninhibited that amazing things come from their honest mouths. Talking with children in a large Philadelphia church I pastored, a child revealed aloud to a crowded church that her mother was a slob around the house. When I asked her what made her say that, she said that's what her dad said.

Here are some other cute ones I have collected and others have shared with me. A kindergarten pupil told his teacher he'd found a cat, but it was dead.

"How do you know that the cat was dead?" she asked her pupil.

"Because I pissed in its ear and it didn't move," answered the child innocently.

You did WHAT?!?" the teacher exclaimed in surprise.

"You know,"explained the boy, "I leaned over and went 'Pssst!' and it didn't move."

A little boy was always getting into mischief. His mother finally asked him "How do you expect to get into Heaven?"

The boy thought it over and said, "Well, I'll run in and out and in and out and keep slamming the door until St. Peter says, 'For Heaven's sake, Dylan, come in or stay out!'"

One summer evening during a violent thunderstorm a mother was tucking her son into bed. She was about to turn off the light when he asked with a tremor in his voice, "Mommy, will you sleep with me tonight?"

His mother smiled, gave him a reassuring hug and said," I can't dear," I have to sleep in Daddy's room."

A long silence was broken by his shaky little voice: "The big sissy."

During one children's sermon one little girl was wearing a particularly pretty dress and, as she sat down, the pastor leaned over and said, "That is a very pretty dress. Is it your Easter Dress?"

The little girl replied, directly into the pastor's clip-on microphone," Yes, and my Mom says it's a bitch to iron."

One woman was six months pregnant with her third child, when her three year old came into the room as she was getting into the shower. She said, "Mommy, you are getting fat!"

The woman replied, "Yes, honey, remember Mommy has a baby growing in her tummy."

"I know," she replied, but what's growing in your butt?"

One day the first grade teacher was reading the story of Chicken Little to her class. She came to the part of the story where Chicken Little tried to warn the farmer. She read, "…. and so Chicken Little went up to the farmer and said, "The sky is falling, the sky is falling!"

The teacher paused then asked the class, "And what do you think that farmer said?"

One little girl raised her hand and said, "I think he said: 'Holy Moly! A talking chicken!'"

Adios

Don't Miss These Books by Vernon Schmid

Rags—A ten part western serial digitally published on-line by Amazon.com/shorts. $4.90.

Waties Wolves: A Novel of the Civil War in Indian Territory
ISBN 978-0-595-89138-2 Hardback. 172 Pages. $23.95.
ISBN 978-0-595-44126-6 Trade Paperback. 172 Pages. $13.95.

Cherokee Myth and Legend.
ISBN 0-7414-3499-7 Trade Paperback. Pages. $13.95.

Otium Sanctum: Poems for the Journey Toward
ISBN 0-7414-3124-6 Trade Paperback. 121 Pages. $11.95.

Westering: New and Selected Poems, 1974-2004
ISBN 0-7414-2661-7 Trade Paperback. 105 Pages. $11.95.

Houlihans and Horse Sense
ISBN 1-4134-4468-7 Trade Paperback. 152 Pages. $20.99.

Showdown at Chalk Creek: A Novel of the Old West
ISBN 1-4134-3625-0 Hardback. 135 Pages. $30.99.
Trade Paperback. 135 Pages. $20.99.

Seven Days of the Dog
ISBN 1-4134-0799-4 Hardback. 193 Pages. $30.99.
ISBN 1-4010-9419-8 Trade Paperback. 193 Pages. $20.99.

Kissing Moctezuma's Serpent
ISBN 0-89002-365-4 Trade Paperback. 54 Pages. $12.95.

Hog Killers and Other Poems
ISBN 0-89002-349-2 Trade Paperback. 45 Pages. $13.95.

978-0-595-46909-3
0-595-46909-4